MW00399300

Making $500,000 A Year In Mail Order

David Bendah

This publication is designed to provide accurate and authoritative information in regard to the subject matter covered. It is sold with the understanding that the publisher is not engaged in rendering legal, accounting, or other professional service. If legal advice or other expert assistance is required, the services of a competent professional should be sought.

Copyright © 1985 by Lion Publishing Company. All rights reserved. Printed in the United States of America. No part of this book may be used or reproduced in any manner whatsoever without written permission except in the case of brief quotations embodied in critical articles or review.

For information, write
P.O. Box 151034, San Diego, CA 92115.

Bendah, David
Making $500,000 A Year In Mail Order.
Library of Congress Catalog Card No. 85-090841

ISBN 0-933301-05-7

This book was typeset by Typecast Graphics of San Diego.

To Julie

Acknowledgements

For their continued support and involvement in the production of this book I would like to thank

Michele Howard
Lorie Hambly

Contents

1

A Secret That Will Make You Rich

I have a secret to share with you, one that will show you how you can make a lot of money in mail order. You can do it because this book is your guide to success. Many self-made millionaires have used the systems in this book to make their fortunes. You can now do the same.

Because you have bought my book and are reading it, the secret is yours — yours to use to make your own fortune. If you are poor, as I once was, this secret will make you rich; if you are already rich, this secret will make you richer.

You can drive a Mercedes convertible, swim in your own pool or live in a house on the sandy seashore. Your search is over. You have just found what you have always sought. You are on your way to the big money you always wanted, and this book is the key. I will explain to you a step-by-step formula that has, without fail, created wealth for some of the wealthiest people on earth.

My secret will change your life. It will help you get whatever you want, and more. In addition, you will have the satisfaction and pride of knowing that you did it on your own. You are on the verge of a brave new world, and I will guide you every step of the way. I will show you how I and others created fortunes. I will show you how to do the same, how you can ensure and enjoy tremendous success while at the same time calling your own shots in your own business. But, above all, you will have the freedom to spend time with your loved ones and on your hobbies and the pleasures life has to offer.

There Is Magic In Belief

A wise man once told me that you will never get rich if you work for someone else. The only way to get rich is by having a vested interest in a business — you must be taking in a share of the profits. You do want to be a millionaire, don't you? There aren't enough days in a year or years in a lifetime for most people to become millionaires while working for others. On their own, though, they can do it in remarkably short order.

So how much money do you want? Name your figure: $2,000? $20,000? $200,000? How about $2 million? When Joe Karbo started out, he wanted a comfortable life; instead, he made a fortune.

Several years ago, Karbo was far worse than broke. He owed more than $50,000 and, he said, his only assets were his wife and eight children. He was renting an old house in a decaying neighborhood, driving a broken-down car and had only a couple of hundred dollars in the bank.

But Karbo believed; he had faith in himself. And because of that faith, he made his million. He lived in a beachfront home, and bought (with cash) a $30,000 lakefront cabin in the Washington mountains where he spent whole summers swimming and sailing. He had two boats and a Cadillac. He owned two beachfront condominiums, one in Mexico, the other in Hawaii.

And he only worked about six hours a day, eight or nine months a year. Would you like to work those hours and make that kind of money?

His belief in himself gave him one other thing, more valuable than his property, his stocks and bonds and cash in the bank: freedom to spend time with his family.

How did all this happen, how did Karbo become one of the biggest mail order success stories of the '70s?

In the early 1960s, Karbo and his wife rented and ran a small but very successful all-night television station; the couple was amassing a small fortune. But, due to circumstances beyond his control, Karbo was forced out of the station when it was sold. Suddenly, he found himself thousands of dollars in debt.

Appropriately enough, he wrote, and sold through the mail, *The Power of Money Management,* detailing methods of getting out of debt. It sold very well in a short time — 100,000 copies at $3.95 each

— and gave him the experience to write his mail order masterpiece.

How did he get over his first financial hurdles? How did he arrive on the threshold of a multimillion-dollar mail order empire? Through belief.

As his crowning glory, Karbo wrote, published and sold through the mail the famous *The Lazy Man's Way to Riches,* and in one year sold 173,000 copies at $10 a shot. That adds up to almost $1.75 million.

Since that first year in the early 1970s, *The Lazy Man's Way To Riches,* translated into many languages, has sold in countries all around the globe; sales exceed one million. In addition, he sold more than 100,000 copies, at $3.95 each, of a book on horse race handicapping.

"People think they have to work hard and deprive themselves to make money," Karbo said in an interview with United Press International. "That's the long, hard way and it doesn't work out too often. I'm not saying money is everything, but with it you have some freedom. I can take the afternoon off if I want to. I'm a very happy guy."

Do you want to be happy? Do you want success? Success is yours if you believe. If you believe, if you have faith in my method, you can end up like Joe Karbo.

Of course, success means different things to different people. To some, it means buying a long-desired possession, like a large home by the beach. To others, it means love and friendship. What does success mean to you? Whatever it means — wealth, recognition, freedom — knowing my secret and acting on it will help you achieve it.

What can stop you getting what you want? Only the limitations you put on yourself. How do I know this? Time and again I have seen people who could have done well, but didn't. Do you know why? Because they believed they could not. When you limit your expectations, you limit the amount of money you can make.

I Didn't Believe In Myself

For many years I worked as a busboy and a waiter. I was barely getting by. I had no belief in myself and just didn't think I could make money on my own. It was only when I had belief in myself that I started to excell.

One day I decided I was tired of the 9-to-5 rat race. I put together a book on saving money at home and called it *Financial Success.* I was able to scrape up a few hundred dollars and began to create my first ad. I designed it carefully and bought ad space in a magazine. I waited for results.

It was a sunny Monday afternoon. I ran home to my mailbox to see if anyone was interested in my $6 book. When I got to the mailbox, I couldn't believe my eyes. It was so stuffed with letters that the mailbox door wouldn't close and I had trouble carrying them all. Each envelope contained a check. I spent four hours opening my mail.

I just couldn't believe I could make so much money in so little time, but the evidence lay in front of me.

Why didn't I make so much money earlier in my life? Why didn't I make money the lazy man's way? The mistake was mine for not believing in myself.

Let me ask you a question: Do you believe in yourself? I urge you to follow this simple advice: BELIEVE IN YOURSELF. Don't go through life making peanuts when you should be making cashews. The choice is yours.

Belief, in yourself and in my secret. You may be skeptical and asking yourself: "Why should I believe?" I ask you this one question: "Why shouldn't you?" You have nothing to lose. I guarantee your success. Learn my secret, the same secret that made millionaires out of people just like you. Follow my program, and you will do well. If you don't try it, your life will not change. Is that what you want? I am giving you the chance of a lifetime.

Most people feel they will go nowhere in life; they lack motivation. Good intentions don't move you ahead unless you have a vehicle. But you are different, you have the vehicle — this book and your belief in yourself. You see that pinpoint of light at the end of the tunnel and you move toward it in large, confident strides — without fearing the dark, without turning back, without doubting yourself.

Do You Have The Desire To Be Rich?

First, you must have the desire to be rich. Not just a normal, everyday desire, but a burning, all-consuming desire. A desire that makes you want to become rich so badly you are willing to learn new ideas, accept new ways, strike out on your own and reach that light at the end of the tunnel. Do you have such a desire? I know you do, because only a person with this desire would buy this book. Your desire to get ahead will get you ahead.

A Man Who Had The Desire

A few years ago, Mark Oliver Haroldson had only $7,000 to his name, but he believed. Now, he is worth more than $5.5 million. He hopes to make millions more and, no doubt, he will.

How? Through belief.

But life was not always rosy for the Haroldsons. Several years ago, he writes, they lived in Denver, Colorado, paying $135 a month for a cramped, run-down house. His wife was expecting their second child, and he had to borrow $300 from his father and father-in-law just to put food on the table and keep the landlord off his back. Times were rough, but Haroldson had faith.

Not faith in his education — he could tell you that age, handicap, even brains, have little to do with success. Teenagers, senior citizens, people with handicaps or little formal education — all have an equal chance of realizing and living their dreams.

Take Haroldson, who graduated with a C-average from Ames High School in Ames, Iowa.

Haroldson started out by investing in real estate. But he saw a way to make even more money, to multiply his worth.

He wrote and published *How to Wake the Financial Genius Inside You*. In a short time, he sold 350,000 mail order copies at $10 each — that adds up to $3.5 million. But without belief in himself, in what he was trying to do, he would only be where he started, back in a tumble-down house and several thousand dollars in debt.

Examine Your Own Beliefs

I urge you to examine your beliefs. Do you have any that are negative? How do you feel about people or any relationships you have? How do you feel about money and other material things? What are your beliefs toward happiness and love?

Examine your beliefs. Sit down and look at yourself carefully, then ask: "What am I like? What do I believe in? Do I truly believe I will be rich?" Just being able to see yourself can help you recognize beliefs you should keep and those you should discard or change.

Ask yourself another question. Ask: "Why am I this way?" This will start you thinking about the reasons your beliefs are the way they are. When you know, you can work on them. To succeed, you must believe, just as Mark Oliver Haroldson believed, just as Arthur Frommer, the self-publisher of *How To See Europe on $5 a Day,* who now owns hotels around the world, believed.

As the old proverb says, "Believe you have it, and you have it." If others like Karbo and Haroldson did it, if I did it, so can you, so will you — if you believe.

How To Wake Up The Financial Genius Inside You.

"I Have Helped More Than 250,000 People Discover Exactly How To Achieve Financial Freedom."

Mark O. Haroldsen became a millionaire in four years because he found a way to harness inflation to his benefit. Now it's your turn! *"I've found"* says Haroldsen, *"that most people just need a specific road map to follow... they can do what I've done."*

THE DIFFERENCE

If hours, efforts, or brains are not what separate the rich from the average guy who is swamped with debts and very little income then what is?

I learned the answer to that question from an old fellow in Denver. This fellow worked in a drug store stocking the shelves. Very few people knew that he had $200,000 in the bank, all of which he had earned starting from nothing.

Within a year after meeting him, I was told and shown the same thing by a young man who had recently earned over a million dollars. By this time, I began to realize that what I was being shown was truly a remarkable and workable way to grow rich.

THE BEGINNING

I began to apply the principles and methods I had been shown. The results were amazing. I couldn't believe how easy it was, in fact it seemed too easy.

But then I met an elderly lady (83 years old) who, although not very smart, has made $117,000 using the same formula.

I then figured my beginning wasn't luck.

For three and one half years, I worked hard to refine and improve on the formula that I had been shown, so that it would be easy to get quicker results.

As I did this, my assets multiplied very rapidly (160% per year) to the point that I didn't have to work any longer.

MORE LEISURE

I guess I am bragging now, but I did start spending a lot of time in our back yard pool, traveling around the country, and doing a lot of loafing.

Then one day a friend asked me how he could do what I had done.

So I began to outline the formula that I had improved to show him really how simple it was, and how he could do the same thing.

By the next time he approached me, I had written almost a complete volume on the easy way for him to copy my results.

EASY TO READ

I wrote this in simple, straight-forward language so anyone could understand it.

This time my friend's questions were very specific. (He had already begun buying properties with the formulas I had been giving him.) Now he had a property he wanted to buy, but was out of cash. How could he buy it?

I not only showed him how to buy without cash, but by the time the deal was complete, he had $5,000 cash in his pocket to boot.

I also showed him how to buy a $26,000 property for $75 down.

ANYONE CAN

You can do exactly what I did, or my close friends have done; in fact, you may well do it better. (I began doing this in my spare time only.)

It doesn't matter where you live or the size of your town or city, my formula will show you exactly how to:

- Buy income properties for as little as $100 down.
- Begin without any cash.
- Put $10,000 cash in your pocket each time you buy (without selling property.)
- Double your assets every year.
- Legally avoid paying federal or state income taxes.
- Buy bargains at ½ their market value.
- Allow you to travel one week out of every month.

When you send me a check or money order for $10, I will send you all my formulas and methods, and you are free to use them anywhere and as often as you would like.

One of many unsolicited comments on my material:

"... when it came I read it. Then I read it again, and have read it about once a week since it came. No magic. No secrets. A plain, easy-to-understand, 1-2-3 way for anybody with a little patience and common sense to become totally independent within a reasonable length of time. The one book I've been looking for for at least fifteen years..."

—Jerry Donaho, Valdez, Alaska

IT'S GUARANTEED

Now if you were a personal friend of mine, I know you would believe me and not need any kind of guarantee, but since you don't know me personally, I will guarantee that you will be completely satisfied and that my formula will work for you if you apply it. I will back up that guarantee by not cashing your check for 30 days, and if you for any reason change your mind, let me know and I will send your uncashed check back.

You may ask, why am I willing to share my formula for wealth? Well, simply because those of you who order my material will be helping to increase my net worth.

You shouldn't care if I profit as long as you profit. I guarantee that you'll be satisfied that my methods will help you or I'll send your money back!

"FINANCIAL FREEDOM"

To order, simply take any size paper, write the words "Financial Freedom", and send your name and address, along with a check for $10.00 to Mark O. Haroldsen, Inc., Dept. MM 2612 So. 1030 West, Salt Lake City, Utah 84119.

If you send for my materials now, I will also send you documents that will show you precisely how you can borrow from $20,000 to $200,000 at 2% above the prime rate using just your signature as collateral.

By the way, if you feel a little uneasy about sending me a check or money order for $10.00, simply postdate it by 30 days which will completely eliminate your risk.

*M3 © Mark O. Haroldsen, Inc. 1978

Inquire at your local bookstore for Mark Haroldsen's "How to Wake Up the Financial Genius Inside You."

Figure 1.1: Mark Haroldson's full-page ad

Take A Chance

What you risk is your time and effort; what you gain is wealth and freedom. Venturing out on a whole new path may scare you a bit, but I will tear you free of your fear of success or whatever else it is that holds you back from enjoying the finer things life has to offer.

Remember what President Franklin D. Roosevelt said: "The only thing we have to fear is fear itself." How right he was!

The only reason you limit yourself is fear, fear of rejection or loss. It is one of the greatest demotivators.

But failure is also one of the best teachers. Every time I suffer a setback, I pick myself up. First I figure out why I fell, then I push forward stronger than before. The truth is that failure helps me learn. If you learn the lessons of your failures, you will become a better person; you will also get rich. The Hindus say that "you will make the same mistake over and over again until you learn your lesson." Learn from failure — it's a great teacher.

Not that self-publishers expect failure, they just know that they must take a chance if they want wealth.

One author took a risk and found success. He wrote a pamphlet on special dental instrumentation, self-published it at 98 cents each and sold it for $10 a copy to 5,000 dentists. That adds up to $50,000.

They Took A Chance

Ken Blanchard and Spencer Johnson of San Diego, California, also took a chance, and theirs is quite a success story. They knew that this is the age of information, that large computer companies and corporations like AT&T know that, above all, their task is to process and provide information. Never before has so much information been available to so many people at such speed, and never before have so many people needed that information so quickly.

Blanchard and Johnson knew that, so they took a chance. But it wasn't that much of a risk, because they believed in themselves and in their product.

Their risk paid off. They self-published the *One Minute Manager* in 1982. The first 5,000 copies of the slim, 119-page book soon sold out, at $15.95 a shot. Due to its success, the publishing company of Morrow and Co. bought rights to the book and now more than 3 million copies have been printed. As if that wasn't success enough, another publisher bought Johnson's second book, the *One Minute Parent*.

Self-publishing, in this age of information and communication, has made money for people just like you. Look at Karbo — before his success, how different was he from you?

Baja Haha

Meet Fred Hoctor, an average guy. He self-published *Baja HaHa,* a light-hearted guide through the Baja California desert country just south of San Diego, California. He is one of a determined band of self-publishers who have made it through hard work and belief in their efforts. Hoctor sold more than 24,000 copies of *Baja Haha* and, a year after publication, the volume is still on bookstore racks.

All these self-publishers, whether they wrote their own material or bought books through mail order companies to sell themselves, know that wealth is a choice. I've asked you this already: How wealthy do you want to be? Name your figure: $2,000? $20,000? $200,000? How does $2 million sound? Pretty good, I'd say.

2

A Business That Will Make You A Fortune

What is the key, the secret, to all the success stories I've told you about? How did Karbo, Haroldson, Johnson and many others strike it rich?

Through self-publishing and selling by mail.

They had an idea, carried it through, and reaped the rewards. You, too, can sow the same seeds and reap the same rewards.

The Legend Of Karbo

With no backing from the big publishing houses, Joe Karbo self-published *The Lazy Man's Way to Riches.* In one year he sold 173,000 copies at $10 each. That's a cool $1.73 million. He also sold more than 100,000 copies of a book on horse race handicapping and the same number of a book called *The Power of Money Management* at $3.95 a shot. That's almost $400,000.

But he didn't stop there. He knew that English is one of the world's most widely used languages and reasoned that a huge market must exist outside the United States. So he made plans to distribute 400,000 copies in England — an additional $4 million in sales potential.

He was right, of course. A huge market for material written in English does exist, both inside and outside this country — in Canada, Europe, Australia, even in Africa. You, too, can tap into this market

They Did It

- Mark Oliver Haroldson self-published *How to Wake the Financial Genius Inside You.* Soon, he had sold 350,000 copies for $10 each through mail order — that adds up to $3.5 million in the bank.

- Ken Blanchard and Spencer Johnson self-published *One Minute Manager;* the first 5,000 copies sold out quickly at $15.95 each. That equals almost $80,000. Soon after, another run of 15,000 copies was printed and sold, making total profits for just the initial printings almost $320,000.

  But the book, after the rights were bought by a publishing company, has sold nearly 3 million copies.

- Marsha Hootman and Patt Perkins self-published *Making the Break* in 1982, which was designed to help people make changes in their lives. They then self-published *How to Forgive Your Ex-Husband and Get On With Your Life,* and took it to an agent. The agent sold it to Doubleday in 1983.

  Impressed, Doubleday gave them a $100,000 advance for their next book, *Change Your Life in Seven Days.* Now they are writing a book, *New Renaissance Woman,* a portrait of women who take total responsiblity for their lives.

A Great Opportunity

This is a good opportunity for you. If a small or large publisher is interested in your book, the firm may purchase the rights from you. A publisher may also give you a cash advance on your next book — Doubleday gave Hootman and Perkins $100,000. How would you like to get paid in advance?

Having your self-published book bought by a publishing and distribution house is very lucrative, and you don't need a lucky break.

Johnson, who co-wrote *One Minute Manager,* planned from the start to have the book bought by a publishing company. After Morrow & Co. bought the book, it sold nearly 3 million copies. Because of this success, Johnson's next book, *One Minute Parent,* was bought at the start by a publishing house.

Whenever you see photographs of these authors on their book covers, they are always smiling. Now you know why.

You can wear the same smile while you march to the bank. All you need is an idea, a touch of ambition, and you're on your way.

As these success stories tell you, never before has there been such a demand for information and how-to books, and never before have there been such profits available through self-publishing and selling books by mail.

Publishing your own how-to books on any one of the infinite number of subjects that interest people can be a very profitable and continuous source of income.

The Boom Is On

You can see the boom in the self-publishing and mail order business all around you, in big display ads (like the one I use for this book), in full book racks and on television talk shows.

Some self-publishers, like some of those I've talked about, write on subjects they know a great deal about. You should do the same. Do friends frequently ask you about a certain subject? Can you cook, garden or fish well? Do you know of a system to save time or money? This is all you need to write a book. Self-publishers make thousands of dollars on information manuals that cost less than 50 cents to produce. They make a very good living, entirely by mail. Isn't it about time you entered this lucrative market?

To show you how the market for these self-published books is booming: Publishers of just three or more books increased from 960 in 1972 to more than 1,500 in 1980, and the increase in publishers of newsletters was double that.

Take Peder Lund, who runs Paladin Press out of Boulder, Colorado. He has sold 8,000 copies of *Silencers, Snipers and Assassins* at $15.95 a shot and 9,000 copies of *The Knife Digest*. But that is only part of his success. Specializing in books on military science, self-defense, wilderness survival and weapons, he issues about 20 books a year, netting him $500,000 in sales annually. More than half his business is generated through magazine advertising, the rest through sales to wholesalers, retailers and libraries.

Why Self-Publish?

So, apart from the huge profits you can make, why should you self-publish?

First, you are your own boss. You make the decisions. In self-publishing, you work at your own pace and for how many hours a day you wish. And when the profits start rolling in, you will have the freedom to spend your increased leisure time anyway you want.

Second, you will not fork over your life savings to a vanity press. A vanity press firm charges you an arm and a leg to publish your book, work you can easily do on your own — in other words, you get a lot less product for a lot more money. In addition, there is a stigma attached to vanity press books, because the author must pay the firm to publish his work. Vanity press books tell the potential buyer that the book was not good enough to be published on its own merits. No such stigma or bad reputation need exist with self-published books.

Third, you avoid the frustration and possible rejection of approaching a big-time publisher — there is probably little chance of a giant distribution firm accepting your first manuscript. Even if your book is accepted, you have to be happy with a measly 5% royalties on sales. The other 95% goes to middlemen.

But when you self-publish, 100 percent of the profits — every penny — is yours. What more motivation do you need?

In addition, you don't have to sell anyone on the merits of your book to get it published, because everything you need to know about printing and marketing it is in this book.

Fourth, you, instead of someone else, has the final say on the quality of your work. Authors who publish through large firms often have their wishes ignored by the publishing house. When you self-publish, you are the quality-control officer and can make sure your book lives up to your personal standards. Also, you are free to make the book any length you like, can experiment with art work and typefaces and can vary page width and depth.

Fifth, you have a tremendous opportunity to make friends and enjoy reader response. As a self-publisher, readers will respond directly to you — you'll enjoy the positive feedback and learn from the negative. Also, you will probably have to deal with printers, wholesalers and retailers, so you have ample chance to build strong business ties.

Sixth, when you self-publish and sell by mail, your book has the time it may need to attract a following and continued sales over many years. If your book does not enjoy outstanding sales as soon as it is published, it will not be wisked off the bookstore shelves at the whim of a large distributor or store owner. Lots of books have little impact when they first come out, but become very profitable as word of mouth travels.

Do you see the advantages of self-publishing and mail order selling? You may think that you have nothing to write about, or that subjects that interest you will not interest others. Wrong. Very wrong.

Here are some self-published book titles, old and new, that indicate the endless variety of salable subjects: *How To Prosper Dur-*

ing the Coming Bad Years, Dress For Success, Never Cooked Before Cookbook, How to Get Out of Debt and *Decorating.*

I Did It

Or, to use one of my highly successful books as an example (and if I can do it, so can you): *The Complete Guide to Getting Grants and Low-Interest Loans.* The first year this book was out, I sold 7,000 copies at $6 each. The second year, 11,000. Sales go up every year. One of my most recent books, *How To Use Your Hidden Potential To Get Rich,* is very successful — in fact, I sold about 1,000 copies at $11 a crack the first month the book was out. That put $11,000 in my pocket.

I now sell 12 books, all by mail order. Some of my titles sell up to 1,500 copies a month. Each one is a breadwinner for me. You can do the exact same thing. If you care to make the journey into profitable mail order self-publishing, it's up to you. If you want to take that journey, I will guide you all the way.

If you would like to see the light at the end of the tunnel, let me show you how to take the first step toward it. Read and study this book — it will show you everything you have to know to make big money in mail order.

3

Planting The Roots Of Success

Setting up a profitable operation is your first step. You will learn how to make a lot of money while keeping all your expenses down.

Don't rent office space (unless you get handed a deal you can't refuse) until you are well established and making a lot of money. Rent is an unnecessary expense. All you need is a quiet little corner in your house, such as your bedroom, basement, attic, garage or kitchen — anywhere you can work without interruption for the few hours a day needed to make money selling books by mail. Find such a place.

There are a few benefits to setting up your mail order business in your home. One is the tax break. I'll go into this tax break more later on, but if you use one room as an office and operate your business out of your home, you can deduct from your taxes some of your rent or mortgage as well as your utility bills.

When I started selling my first book, *Financial Success,* my bedroom was my office and my kitchen was my shipping department. I placed a small filing cabinet in my closet, a working table and typewriter beside my bed.

A checking account is important. If you haven't already opened one, do so. Paying by check is the easiest way to pay your bills. The cancelled checks, which you should keep for seven years, provide proof of purchase, essential should you be the target of a tax audit.

Also, it is much easier to itemize your expenses with a checking account. Itemizing expenses at the end of the year helps you analyze your business's performance, important for efficiency. If you pay cash for any service or supplies, make sure you get and keep a receipt. Remember, most business expenses are tax deductible, and cancelled checks and receipts prove to the tax man you've paid them.

Believe me, I know from experience. When I started out, I didn't have a checking account and made all my purchases with cash and money orders. Then, when I finally did get a checking account, people wouldn't accept my checks because I didn't have a credit card. The worse thing about the way I delt with bills was how I itemized my expenses for April 15. It was terrible. I had a receipt here, one there and lots I didn't know where. Don't let the same happen to you. Keep good records and study Chapter 16.

Types of Business Organization

There are three forms your mail order, self-publishing business can take: sole proprietorship, partnership or corporation. Each has advantages and disadvantages.

Sole proprietorship

This is the simplest, cheapest and most common, and allows you to run the business pretty much as you wish (there are no board of directors or partners to satisfy).

You do not need a special license to sell books (unlike other businesses) so all you have to do is go to your city or county clerk and pay $25 or less for a business license. If you do business under your own name, there are no additional costs. Also, with a sole proprietorship, you save on legal fees because, unlike with corporations and partnerships, no contracts are needed.

As a sole proprietorship, you enjoy a major tax break: The government considers you and your business as one. If you have a full-time job and are running your mail order business part time, this is especially good news because you can deduct business losses from any other source of income. For other tax breaks, contact your local IRS branch office.

In addition, as a sole proprietorship, you may keep your financial records on a cash or accrual basis. Cash-basis record keeping is easier, lets you defer income and demands less bookkeeping; accrual-basis record keeping may be better for you when you grow into a large company.

The one chief disadvantage, however, is that in any legal action, you and your business are one — you have unlimited personal liablity. If your company is sued or fails financially while owing creditors, the personal assets you own outside your business can be sold to meet your debts.

Also, you may be at a disadvantage when trying to borrow money. Lending institutions and investors are more comfortable lending to a partnership than to a solo effort, because they can rely on more than one person to pay the money back.

Partnership

Business consultants commonly slam the idea of partnerships — they are thought to have all the disadvantages of a marriage with none of the advantages. But there are sound reasons why a partnership may be for you.

The first is that two heads are better than one. A partner will have different skills than you and add to the total talent on which your business depends. Say you have the knack of writing ad copy and he, an accountant, knows a few marketing techniques — the sum is greater than the parts.

And not only might your partner be a source of capital, he will also make it easier for you to take vacations.

As with a sole proprietorship, you need a business license (again, about $25) from the city or county clerk. With the IRS, you must file Form 1065, U.S. Partnership Return of Income, each year. Remember to deduct any losses the partnership suffers from another source of income.

A major disadvantage of the partnership, however, is that two heads may not be better than one: Make sure you and your partner are compatible before investing time and money in the venture. This means more than just getting along OK on a casual basis. Before anything else, you and your partner(s) must decide who will perform and have the responsibility for which tasks. You must work out how decisions will be made, who will make them and who has the final say. The agreement should be sealed by a contract drawn up with the help of any attorney.

As a partner, you are responsible for your partner's decisions, whether or not you help make them. If he makes a bad business decision or skips off to Mexico with the year's profits, you still must face the creditors. In addition, just as with a sole proprietorship, you are personally liable for any lawsuits or financial claims made against your business.

If keeping total control of your business is important to you, consider taking in limited partners. They invest in your company but have nothing to do with the day-to-day running of the business. With this method you can raise large amounts of capital in a short time without using your own money.

In contrast to the limited partner is the general partner — a full partner who is personally liable beyond the extent of his investment, participates day to day and often receives a salary.

A common and successful way to start a mail order self-publishing business is to be a general partner yourself and attract capital by offering limited partnerships.

Corporation

There are major advantages to forming a corporation, but, for a small mail order self-publishing operation, they are probably outweighed by the disadvantages.

The biggest advantage is that you are not personally liable beyond the amount of your investment. Corporations are separate legal entitites: They can be sued but their stockholders cannot. If your book is unlikely to prompt law suits, which can be voided by a published disclaimer, this in not much of an advantage. The type of books that are often the targets of law suits are those on diet and nutrition. If you intend to publish this type of book and value your personal property, consider forming a corporation.

Another advantage is that corporations pay taxes on a maximum of 48% of net profits, whereas personal income is taxed up to 90%. If you reinvest this saved tax money and sell your business when it is large, you pay capital gains tax, not personal income tax, which is higher.

The major disadvantage of a corporation is all the paperwork and other corporate-related activities that are required by law and closely regulated. A corporation must have a board of directors, hold stockholders' meetings, publish minutes, meet payroll taxes and pay an annual registration fee (in California, $200).

One of the three business formats will suit you the best, so choose wisely and consult a variety of free or inexpensive booklets. Write to the Small Business Administration, Washington, D.C., 10414, and request publications dealing with starting a small business. Also, write to Bank of America Marketing Publications, P.O. Box 37000, San Francisco, CA 94137, and request a copy of *Steps to Starting a Small Business.*

Taxes

Many people make a great living with small mail order operations, but only because they know how to get back every penny possible from Uncle Sam.

Apart from being able to deduct losses against income from another source, authors and publishers get other breaks. For example, you can deduct the cost of printing and advertising your book, expenses you met while writing it, the cost of travel to promote it, to go to book fairs, etc. Also, a portion of your utilities and mortgage may be deductible.

Buy a copy of the *Small Business Tax Guide* at your nearest IRS office.

In addition to federal and state income taxes, there are two types of state taxation that concern you: use tax and sales tax.

A use tax is paid to the state in which your place of business is located; sales tax is paid by the customer to the state in which the purchase is made.

Use tax

Use tax is a complicated issue — problems arise because each state has a different definition of "place of business" and because your mail order business spans state lines. Some states try to tax direct marketers regardless of in which state the business is located. Contact your local state office for more information.

Sales tax

Most states collect a sizable sales tax. For example, the sales tax in California is 6%. You must collect the required sales tax on orders that are not for resale by another dealer and that are sent to addresses within your state. Many of your books will be sold in other states, which gives mail order a sales tax advantage.

As a business, to avoid collecting sales tax on each order, you must prove that the shipping address on the invoice is out of state, or the books must be for resale. You may have to keep a record of customer resale numbers; you may have to send a standard resale number request card with the invoice to the appropriate state tax office, listed in Chapter 4.

A useful hint: Get your resale permit (discussed in Chapter 4) before your book is printed. That way, you avoid paying your printer sales tax when your book is delivered.

Budgeting Your Business

You are in business to make a profit. Profit is the name of the game. Without it, your mail order business is merely an expensive hobby, a tax write-off or a waste of time.

You're playing this game to make money, so you must plan your strategy with care. I will show you a proven strategy that has given me excellent results.

It is impossible to state how much money you need to start a mail order book business, because you can start with as much or as little as you like. It is best to start small, expanding as you improve your feel for mail order.

Mail order is unique because you get paid before you ship the product out. You don't have to worry about not getting paid and collecting money; you will grow and flourish in a relatively short time.

The best way to figure your minimum investment is to add up all initial costs, such as letterheads, office supplies and sales literature. They will probably be about $100.

Add to this the cost of three months worth of advertising, which you can find out by contacting various magazines. While you should budget enough for three months advertising, only buy one month of advertising space. This way, you can test your ad before entering a full-scale campaign.

If the one ad you place is successful, place more, paid for by the two extra months advertising for which you originally budgeted.

Notice that you do not include the cost of producing the books you plan to sell by mail. Why not? Because, as I will elaborate on later, you will have no production costs if you take advantage of drop-shipping, an attractive and lucrative starting point for the beginner with little cash.

When you drop-ship, you order a ready-made product, such as a book, and fill orders as they come in. With this method, you have no book-storage problems and no money tied up in inventory.

If, however, you have plenty of cash and are experienced in mail order, you should have little worry about producing and selling your own book. I started out with drop-shipping, but now I publish and store all my books.

If you do decide to produce your own book, you will have such expenses as storage and printing.

Keep a record of all the money you take in for the initial three-month period; figure out your profit merely by subtracting all your costs.

A simple and standard budget formula is:

Dollars taken in though sales - all costs = net profit.

A few words of wisdom: Don't start your business on borrowed money. Don't take undue financial risk by taking out a short-term, high-interest loan. Don't cash in an insurance policy to get started. Think twice about selling any real capital to finance your venture. Always use money you can spare. If you do this, you should be safe.

After your business is off the ground and flying, that is the time to borrow money to expand.

Your Equipment

First, get a desk. The bigger the desk, the more drawers and working space, the better; but a cheap table with plenty of working surface will do. You can even take over the kitchen table.

You can probably pick up a filing cabinet for $40 to $90, or use a cardboard accordion file. Good business records increase the efficiency of your company as well as organize it, and good organization means big dollars.

Next, you need a typewriter, either used or new, manual or electric. To cut initial costs, you can rent-to-own a typewriter, rather than buy one. Your typewriter should have a new ribbon and clean keys. As a letter is often your first contact with someone, you should make a good first impression.

To go with the typewriter, you need a correcting tape or white-out liquid to correct inevitable errors.

Of course, to get any use out of your typewriter, you must be able to type. If you can't, take an inexpensive night typing class at your local community college or adult school. If you don't want to learn, you can hire a typist on a per-page basis.

All your correspondence should be typed; handwritten letters can be sloppy, appear unprofessional and unbusinesslike, and will brand you an amateur. I sometimes make an exception to this rule. If a customer sends me a letter that needs a very quick response, I just write my reply on his letter, make a copy of it, then send it back to him.

To be properly organized, you will need shelves to store your stock of books and sales material. An old bookcase will do.

In addition, you will need standard office supplies, such as gummed labels, stapler, staple remover, masking tape, scissors, pens, erasers, etc. You should also have such standard writing tools as a late-edition dictionary and *Roget's Thesaurus.* If you have trouble writing clearly and using correct grammar, Strunk and White's *The*

Elements of Style is a good reference.

All About Telephones

You don't really need a business telephone if you are just starting out in the mail order field. Many people use their home phones. In fact, I didn't have a business phone installed until after I'd been filling orders for three years.

One of the problems with a phone is that customers call you collect, even for a small order. If you accept these calls, down goes your profit margin. I recommend that you use a business phone only if you plan on a large number of sales or if the cost of your books is very high. If you find you are a spending a great deal of time on unprofitable calls, consider an answering service or machine.

Toll-free numbers

In general, the toll-free number service is not cost-effective for mail order, unless you have sales of at least $500,000 a year and accept credit cards. Even if you do have such a large sales volume, to make a toll-free service profitable, your asking price should be high, more than $20 an order.

However, there are times when a toll-free number could be to your advantage. If your display ads mention that a customer can charge an order to his credit card by calling a toll-free number, sales of products priced at more than $15 will greatly increase. In fact, some advertising campaigns that ask for more than $15 would flop without toll-free numbers. This applies even more to television and direct mail advertising.

You don't have to buy a toll-free number line to offer your customers this service. Some toll-free services will let you use their lines and charge you a fee for each call. A typical fee is $1 to $2 a call with a 100-call minimum per month. This works like an answering service.

The National Communications Center offers this service. To find out more about rates and services, call toll free: 800/824-7888; or, from Alaska or Hawaii: 800/824-5180.

Your Company Image

While you should try to keep all costs as low as possible, you should not cut corners on your sales literature or your book production. Remember, since you rarely meet face-to-face with a mail order customer, you do not need to put up a front by purchasing expensive office furniture, etc. But, since the impression your customers get of you is through your sales literature and your final product, do not skimp on letterheads or paper quality.

Just has trying to save money on your sales literature can give your company a cheap, fly-by-night appearance, sparing yourself the effort of thinking up a suitable and catchy name results in an unimaginative, dull image. I am sure you want your customers to be impressed, so I've laid out everything you need to portray a positive, solid business image.

Your name

What's in a name? Everything. As the old proverb goes: "He who has an ill name is half hanged." What this means is that if you don't have a good company name, you're probably dead before you start; that your potential customers will judge your product partly on your name. If what you name your company affects sales, isn't it worth the time and effort to think of a good name and logo?

For example, Lion Publishing Company, the name of the company that published this book. It is powerful, inspires confidence and creates emotional appeal by prompting images of the King of the Jungle. It is also easy to illustrate in an attractive way. And, because the name is short, it keeps the word count low in classified ads.

Of course, you can use your own name, for example: Smith Publishing Company; John Smith Publishers; Smith Book Co. You may hesitate to use your own name if it is hard to pronounce or spell, if is is unusually long, or if it has ethnic connotations. If your name is any of these, you may think it a liability, but you are probably overly concerned — if your service is prompt, your product of high quality and your price right, customers will order from you. Remember, Montgomery Ward and Sears Roebuck decided to use their names.

Whatever you name your company, you must not deceive the public. If your name is John Crown and you sell books, you can call your company John Crown Co.; but if you call it Crown Books, you're in trouble. And, if you use words like "Publishing Company," make sure you really are publishing something.

In the mail order business, words such as "Company" or "Services" added on the end of your business name are OK, even though they don't mean much However, to use "Inc." for "incorporated," your company must be legally incorporated.

Regulations concerning registering your company name vary from state to state and even from city to city — check with your local county or city clerk for all the information you need.

You may have to register your company name as a DBA, or "doing business as," but the cost should be less than $20. This is also called "ficticious name registration," and you probably will have to do it only if the name of your company is not your name. For example, if I use the name "David Bendah" and list my business as "self-publishing and mail order," I would not need to register my business name. But if I use the name "Bendah Publishing Co." or "David Bendah and Associates," I would probably need to register the "fictitious" name.

The form is simple, and the information on it usually must be published in a newspaper within a month of filing, once a week for four weeks in a row. As I said, the initial filing fee will probably be less than $20; but on top of that, the newspaper will charge between $10 and $100 to print the information.

Your logo

All successful companies have a distinct company image, a logotype (logo) that immediately identifies them. How important are logos? NBC paid $750,000 for the "N" logo you see on TV. Expensive, isn't it? NBC was willing to pay that price because the company executives know that a well-designed logo will make money in the long run. You will find that a logo will help people recognize your company and will enhance your professional image.

My company logo is a lion. I didn't have to choose a lion — a fancy L might have done as well. I chose a lion because I have always been intriged by roaring lions. A lion to me is a sign of power.

Your logo should be professionally prepared. Look up graphic designers in the Yellow Pages, call them up and ask what they charge — prices will vary, so shop around. Examine samples of work until you find an artist you like, feel comfortable with and can afford.

If you have a hard time finding someone to create your logo, take advantage of my logo-design service. One of my talented artists will create your artistic, personalized, camera-ready logo for only $15. The logo will be shipped to you within 24 hours; if you are not satisfied with it, send it back and another will be designed at no extra charge. For your logo, send $15 to Lion Publishing Company.

Once you pick a logo, have business letterheads printed. Ask your printer to recommend a quality paper, such as 50 lb. offset or 20 lb. bond. A high-grade, light-weight paper is better than a lower-grade, heavier paper. If you want your letterhead to look impressive, you

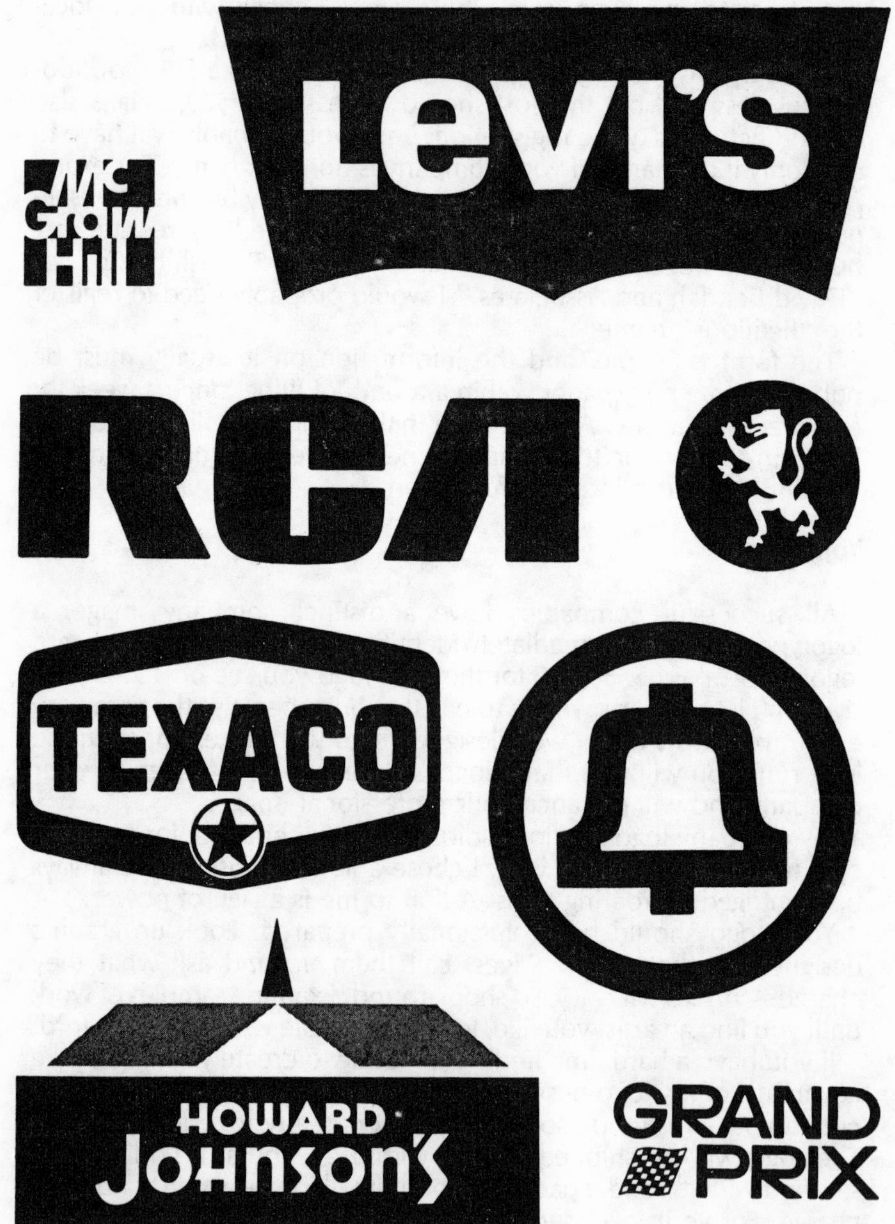

Figure 3.1: Sample logos

can always use more expensive colored paper, such as classic laid or circa.

To go with your letterheads, order envelopes — No. 10 size business envelopes — with your company name, logo and address in the top left corner.

Make sure you really need business cards before you order them. They are not that essential for mail order firms, but if you decide that they will promote your business, try them. The cheapest are of black ink on white card; more expensive and better looking are colored cards and ink, perhaps matching your stationery.

As with all goods and services, prices vary, so shop around and look for the best deal.

Box number vs. street address

You may be concerned about using your home, P.O. Box or office address in your ads.

One the one hand, you may fear customers will come to your home to check out your book, or even that dissatisfied readers will come to your doorstep. On the other hand, you may be worried that a post office box number in your ads will make potential buyers think you are a hit-and-run operation.

California law demands that you run a street address in your ad, regardless of whether you list a post office box as well. People are likely to come to your home or office to check out your book before they buy it — no problem, as long as your book is of good quality. If it is a value, people will buy it on the spot. Most people who come into my office leave with at least a few books.

Here is how I suggest you handle your business address. I have found that the best way to increase your mail is to include a street address, unless you are a well-known company people trust. You don't have to rent an office, just rent a street address. There are many companies that do just that. I rented my first address from an answering service. Most answering services have street address box rentals. Mail Boxes Etc. is a franchise retail outlet that handles mail very well. You should consider them if they are available in your town. If you still can't find a street address, look up "box rentals" in your Yellow Pages. One word of caution: Make sure the place you use for your mail will be around for the next few years.

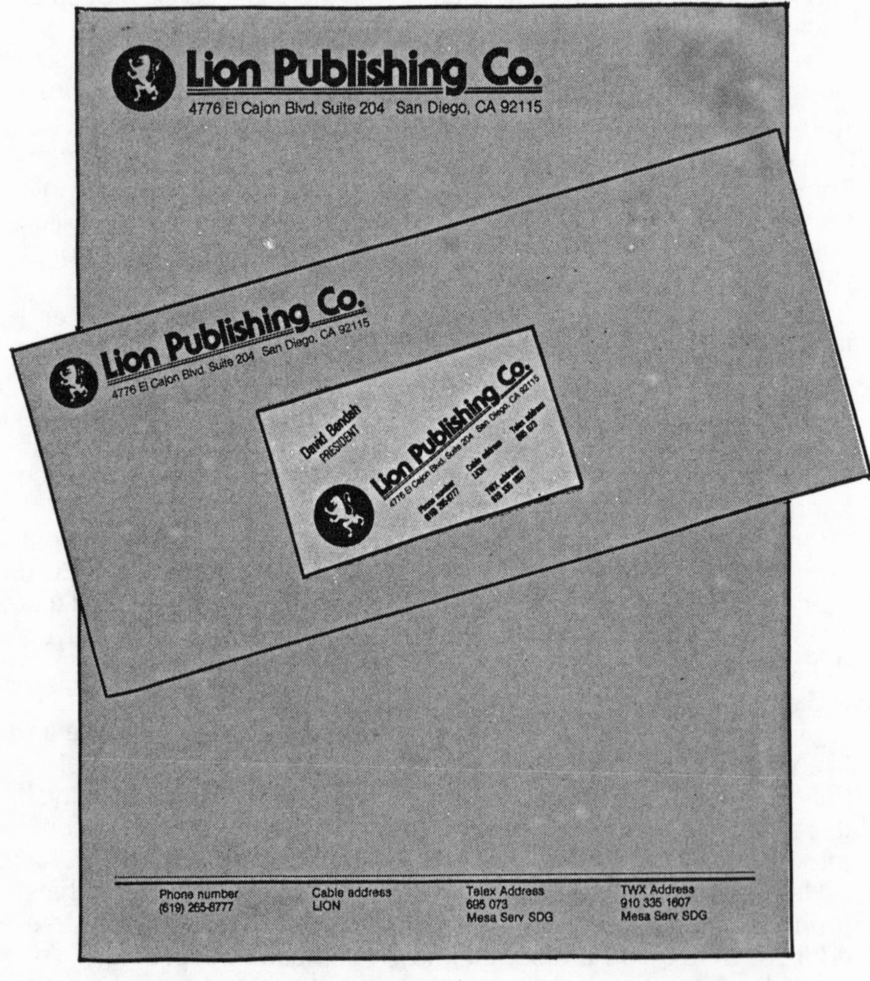

Figure 3.2: My stationery

Increase Your Knowledge of Mail Order

How To Get Rich In Mail Order

There are two books that will help you run your business and add to your knowledge of mail order. To do well, you must learn from those who have made a lot of money doing what you want to do. I recommend only two good books. The first, and one of the best in the field, is *How To Get Rich In Mail Order,* by Melvin Powers. Extensively experienced, Powers has made millions selling more books by mail than any other publishing company in the world. In fact, he sells 400 different titles by mail. I recommend this book because it specializes in mail order book selling.

Powers' book is well written, full of helpful, easy-to-understand information, and is used extensively to teach college students how to master the art of mail order selling. It has 326 8½-by-11-inch pages, and may be found at your local bookstore for $16. If not, send $16 to Lion Publishing and I will mail you a copy within 48 hours, postpaid and insured.

Building A Mail Order Business

The second book I recommend highly is *Building a Mail Order Business, A Complete Manual for Success,* by William Cohen. It is hard bound and 495 pages, and covers every aspect of selling by mail, from the basics to the most sophisticated techniques for increasing sales. Every method is explained in a detailed, logical fashion that shows you, step-by-step, how to do it and do it right.

This is one of the most complete up-to-date mail order guides. Cohen covers product selection, writing, graphics, competition and the legal aspects of mail order. You should be able to pick up this book at your local bookstore for $20. If not, send me $21 and I'll mail you a copy within 48 hours, postpaid and insured.

How To Start, Expand & Sell A Business

A very good book I recommend to my readers is *How To Start, Expand & Sell A Business,* by James Comiskey. Backed by 14 years experience as a business consultant, Comiskey launched what was to become the largest chain of retail pet centers in the Western United States, with sales of $2.5 million. Comiskey, who has made a lot of entrepreneurs wealthy, has gathered all his valuable knowledge into one book. In my opinion, it is very well done, informative and helpful. You can pick up a copy of this 8½-by-11-inch, 265-page book at your local bookstore for $17.95. If you prefer, you can order it from Lion Publishing for only $16, including postage. Your copy will be shipped to you within 48 hours.

4

The Legal Requirements

The various regulations and licenses the state and federal governments require you to follow and purchase are covered throughout this book, but here are the basic licenses you probably will have to obtain, depending on where your business is.

Business license

This is easy to get and is merely a permit granted by the local governing body allowing you to do business. Simply contact the city clerk of the city in which your business operates to see whether you need a business license. If you do, it will probably cost about $25. If you don't live in a city, but in an unicorporated area of a county, contact the county clerk for the same information. The clerk will be able to tell you if a state license or permit is also required, and who at the state office you should contact.

You will have to complete an application, stating your name and the names of any partners, your address, the type of business and other pertinent information. The clerk will tell you if you need the OK of the local police or fire department to get started. You probably won't, since your business is mail order, but you may have to state that you have little inventory on hand.

Seller's permit

In some cases, a seller's permit is required to sell books. Check with the appropriate state office listed below to see if you need one.

Also called a resell permit, a seller's permit issued by the state in which you do business allows you to buy personal property for resell and avoid paying use or sales tax on your purchase.

Rather than pay sales tax to the person you are buying the property from on every purchase you make, you merely give him a resell notice that shows your seller's permit number. Then, you collect the sales tax from your customer and give it to the state.

To get your permit, if you need one, contact the office listed below under your state. You may have to pay a fee; you may also have to offer the state a security to ensure that you forward to the state all the sales tax you collect. The security deposit may be several thousand dollars — the amount is determined by such factors as home ownership, your monthly expenses and whether you have a full-time job and work part time in mail order. Should the state demand too high a security, it is possible to reduce it through negotiation. The only reason the state will ask for a high security deposit is if you expect to pay a lot of tax the first year.

When you apply for a seller's permit, wear casual clothes, tell the state you are just starting out, that most sales will either be to out-of-state addresses or to wholesalers. This will probably make your security very small or zero and will permit you to report once a year instead of four times a year.

Addresses of state sales tax departments

Alabama
Dept. of Revenue
Sales and Use Taxes
Montgomery, AL 36130

Alaska
Dept. of Revenue
Pouch S
Juneau, AK 99801

Arizona
Sales Tax Divison
Phoenix, AZ 85007

Arkansas
Sales and Use Tax Div.
Finance and Administration
Little Rock, AR 72201

California
Dept. of Business Taxes
State Board of Equalization
P.O. Box 1799
Sacramento, CA 95808

Colorado
Dept. of Revenue
State Capitol Annex
Denver, CO 80203

Connecticut
Sales, Use and Excise Tax
Hartford, CT 06115

Delaware
State Div. of Revenue
Wilmington, DE 19801

District of Columbia
Dept. of Finance and Revenue
300 Indiana Ave., N.W.
Washington, D.C. 20001

Florida
Sales Tax Bureau
Dept. of Revenue
Tallahassee, FL 32304

Georgia
Sales and Use Tax Unit
Dept. of Revenue
Atlanta, GA 30334

Hawaii
Dept. of Taxation
State Tax Office Bldg.
425 Queen Street
Honolulu, HI 96813

Idaho
Sales Tax Div.
State Tax Commission
Boise, ID 83707

Illinois
Dept. of Revenue
Springfiled, IL 62706

Indiana
Sales Tax Div.
Dept. of Revenue
100 N. Senate Ave.
Indianapolis, IN 46204

Iowa
Div. of Retail Sales and Use Tax
Dept. of Revenue
Lucas State Office Bldg.
Des Moines, IA 50319

Kansas
Sales and Compensating Tax Div.
State Revenue Bldg.
Dept. of Revenue
Topeka, KS 66612

Louisiana
Collector of Revenue
Baton Rouge, LA 70821

Maine
Sales Tax Div.
Bureau of Taxation
Augusta, ME 04330

Maryland
Retail Sales Tax Div.
Treasury Dept.
301 W. Preston Street
Baltimore, MD 21201

Massachusetts
Sales and Use Taxes
Dept. of Corporation and Taxation
Boston, MA 02133

Michigan
Sales and Use Taxes
Dept. of Treasury
Revenue Div.
Treasury Bldg.
Lansing, MI 48922

Minnesota
Sales and Use Tax Div.
Dept. of Taxation
Centennial Office Bldg.
St. Paul, MN 55101

Mississippi
Sales and Use Tax Div.
State Tax Commission
Jackson, MS 39205

Missouri
Sales and Use Tax Bureau
P.O. Box 840
Jefferson City, MO 65102

Nebraska
Sales and Use Tax Unit
Dept. of Revenue
Box 4818, State Capitol
Lincoln, NE 65809

Nevada
Nevada Tax Commission
Carson City, NV 89701

New Jersey
Div. of Taxation
Dept. of the Treasury
Trenton, NJ 08625

New Mexico
Revenue, Bureau of Revenue
Santa Fe, NM 87501

New York
Sales Tax Bureau
State Tax Commission
Dept. of Taxation and Finance
Tax and Finance Bldg. 9
State Campus
Albany, NY 12226

North Carolina
Sales and Use Tax Div.
Main Office—Revenue Bldg.
Raleigh, NC 27611

North Dakota
Enforcement Director
(Sales Tax)
State Capitol Bldg.
Bismarck, ND 58501

Ohio
Sales and Excise Div.
Dept. of Taxation
68 East Gay Street
Columbus, OH 43151

Oklahoma
Sales and Use Taxes
Oklahoma Tax Commission
2010 Lincoln Blvd.
Oklahoma City, OK 73105

Pennsylvania
Bureau of Taxes for Education
Dept. of Revenue
Harrisburg, PA 17123

Rhode Island
Dept. of Administration
49 Westminister Street
Providence, RI 02903

South Carolina
Sales and Use Tax Div.
South Carolina Tax Commission
Columbia, SC 29201

South Dakota
Sales and Use Tax Div.
Dept. of Revenue
Pierre, SD 57501

Tennessee
Sales and Use Tax Div.
Dept. of Revenue
War Memorial Bldg.
Nashville, TN 37219

Texas
Comptroller of Public Accounts
Austin, TX 78711

Utah
Auditing Div. (Sales Tax)
State Tax Commission
201 State Office Bldg.
Salt Lake City, UT 84114

Vermont
Dept. of Taxes
State of Vermont
P.O. Box 547
Montpelier, VT 05604

Virginia
Sales and Use Tax Div.
Dept. of Taxation
P.O.Box 6L
Richmond, VA 23215

Washington
Dept. of Revenue
Olympia, WA 98501

West Virginia
Sales and Use Taxes
State Tax Dept.
Charleston, WV 25305

Wisconsin
Income, Sales, and Excise Tax Div.
Dept. of Revenue
P.O. Box 39
Madison, WI 53702

Wyoming
Sales and Use Tax Div.
State Tax Commission
Cheyenne, WY 82002

Copyright

What is copyright?

Copyright is a form of protection provided by the laws of the United States to the authors of "original works of authorship" including literary, dramatic, musical, artistic and certain other works. Both published and unpublished works are protected.

Section 106 of the Copyright Act generally gives the owner of the copyright the exclusive right to do and to authorize others to do the following:

- To reproduce the copyrighted work in copies or phonorecords.
- To prepare works based upon the copyrighted work.
- To distribute copies or phonorecords of the copyrighted work to the public by sale or other transfer of ownership, or by rental, lease or lending.
- To perform the copyrighted work publicly, in the case of literary, musical, dramatic and choreographic works, pantomimes, and pictorial, graphic or sculptural works, including the individual images of a motion picture or other audiovisual work.

What is not protected?

Several categories of material are generally not eligible for copyright protection. Among others, these include:

- Works that have not been fixed in a tangible form of expression. For example: choreographic works which have not been notated or recorded, or improvisational speeches or perfomances that have not been written or recorded.
- Titles, names, short phrases and slogans, familiar symbols or designs; mere variations of typographic ornamentation, lettering or coloring; mere listings of ingredients or contents.
- Ideas, procedures, methods, systems, processes, concepts, principles, discoveries or devices, as distingusihed from a description, explanation or illustration.

FORM TX
UNITED STATES COPYRIGHT OFFICE
REGISTRATION NUMBER

TX TXU
EFFECTIVE DATE OF REGISTRATION

Month Day Year

DO NOT WRITE ABOVE THIS LINE. IF YOU NEED MORE SPACE, USE A SEPARATE CONTINUATION SHEET.

1

TITLE OF THIS WORK ▼

PREVIOUS OR ALTERNATIVE TITLES ▼

PUBLICATION AS A CONTRIBUTION If this work was published as a contribution to a periodical, serial, or collection, give information about the collective work in which the contribution appeared. Title of Collective Work ▼

If published in a periodical or serial give: Volume ▼ Number ▼ Issue Date ▼ On Pages ▼

2

a NAME OF AUTHOR ▼ — DATES OF BIRTH AND DEATH Year Born ▼ Year Died ▼

Was this contribution to the work a "work made for hire"? ☐ Yes ☐ No

AUTHOR'S NATIONALITY OR DOMICILE Name of Country OR { Citizen of ▶ / Domiciled in ▶

WAS THIS AUTHOR'S CONTRIBUTION TO THE WORK Anonymous? ☐ Yes ☐ No Pseudonymous? ☐ Yes ☐ No If the answer to either of these questions is "Yes," see detailed instructions

NATURE OF AUTHORSHIP Briefly describe nature of the material created by this author in which copyright is claimed. ▼

b NAME OF AUTHOR ▼ — DATES OF BIRTH AND DEATH Year Born ▼ Year Died ▼

Was this contribution to the work a "work made for hire"? ☐ Yes ☐ No

AUTHOR'S NATIONALITY OR DOMICILE Name of Country OR { Citizen of ▶ / Domiciled in ▶

WAS THIS AUTHOR'S CONTRIBUTION TO THE WORK Anonymous? ☐ Yes ☐ No Pseudonymous? ☐ Yes ☐ No If the answer to either of these questions is "Yes," see detailed instructions

NATURE OF AUTHORSHIP Briefly describe nature of the material created by this author in which copyright is claimed. ▼

c NAME OF AUTHOR ▼ — DATES OF BIRTH AND DEATH Year Born ▼ Year Died ▼

Was this contribution to the work a "work made for hire"? ☐ Yes ☐ No

AUTHOR'S NATIONALITY OR DOMICILE Name of Country OR { Citizen of ▶ / Domiciled in ▶

WAS THIS AUTHOR'S CONTRIBUTION TO THE WORK Anonymous? ☐ Yes ☐ No Pseudonymous? ☐ Yes ☐ No If the answer to either of these questions is "Yes," see detailed instructions

NATURE OF AUTHORSHIP Briefly describe nature of the material created by this author in which copyright is claimed. ▼

NOTE

Under the law, the "author" of a "work made for hire" is generally the employer, not the employee (see instructions). For any part of this work that was "made for hire" check "Yes" in the space provided, give the employer (or other person for whom the work was prepared) as "Author" of that part, and leave the space for dates of birth and death blank.

3

YEAR IN WHICH CREATION OF THIS WORK WAS COMPLETED This information must be given in all cases. ◀ Year

DATE AND NATION OF FIRST PUBLICATION OF THIS PARTICULAR WORK Complete this information ONLY if this work has been published. Month ▶ Day ▶ Year ▶ ◀ Nation

4

COPYRIGHT CLAIMANT(S) Name and address must be given even if the claimant is the same as the author given in space 2.▼

See instructions before completing this space.

TRANSFER If the claimant(s) named here in space 4 are different from the author(s) named in space 2, give a brief statement of how the claimant(s) obtained ownership of the copyright.▼

DO NOT WRITE HERE OFFICE USE ONLY: APPLICATION RECEIVED / ONE DEPOSIT RECEIVED / TWO DEPOSITS RECEIVED / REMITTANCE NUMBER AND DATE

MORE ON BACK ▶ • Complete all applicable spaces (numbers 5-11) on the reverse side of this page. • See detailed instructions. • Sign the form at line 10.

DO NOT WRITE HERE
Page 1 of ____ pages

Figure 4.1: Copyright Form TX

EXAMINED BY

FORM TX

CHECKED BY

☐ CORRESPONDENCE Yes

☐ DEPOSIT ACCOUNT FUNDS USED

FOR COPYRIGHT OFFICE USE ONLY

DO NOT WRITE ABOVE THIS LINE. IF YOU NEED MORE SPACE, USE A SEPARATE CONTINUATION SHEET.

5

PREVIOUS REGISTRATION Has registration for this work, or for an earlier version of this work, already been made in the Copyright Office?
☐ Yes ☐ No If your answer is "Yes," why is another registration being sought? (Check appropriate box) ▼
☐ This is the first published edition of a work previously registered in unpublished form.
☐ This is the first application submitted by this author as copyright claimant.
☐ This is a changed version of the work, as shown by space 6 on this application.
If your answer is "Yes," give: **Previous Registration Number ▼** **Year of Registration ▼**

6

DERIVATIVE WORK OR COMPILATION Complete both space 6a & 6b for a derivative work; complete only 6b for a compilation.
a. Preexisting Material Identify any preexisting work or works that this work is based on or incorporates. ▼

b. Material Added to This Work Give a brief, general statement of the material that has been added to this work and in which copyright is claimed. ▼

See instructions before completing this space

7

MANUFACTURERS AND LOCATIONS If this is a published work consisting preponderantly of nondramatic literary material in English, the law may require that the copies be manufactured in the United States or Canada for full protection. If so, the names of the manufacturers who performed certain processes, and the places where these processes were performed must be given. See instructions for details.
Names of Manufacturers ▼ **Places of Manufacture ▼**

8

REPRODUCTION FOR USE OF BLIND OR PHYSICALLY HANDICAPPED INDIVIDUALS A signature on this form at space 10, and a check in one of the boxes here in space 8, constitutes a non-exclusive grant of permission to the Library of Congress to reproduce and distribute solely for the blind and physically handicapped and under the conditions and limitations prescribed by the regulations of the Copyright Office: (1) copies of the work identified in space 1 of this application in Braille (or similar tactile symbols); or (2) phonorecords embodying a fixation of a reading of that work; or (3) both.
a ☐ Copies and Phonorecords b ☐ Copies Only c ☐ Phonorecords Only

See instructions.

9

DEPOSIT ACCOUNT If the registration fee is to be charged to a Deposit Account established in the Copyright Office, give name and number of Account.
Name ▼ **Account Number ▼**

CORRESPONDENCE Give name and address to which correspondence about this application should be sent. Name Address Apt City State Zip ▼

Area Code & Telephone Number ▶

Be sure to give your daytime phone ◀ number

10

CERTIFICATION* I, the undersigned, hereby certify that I am the
Check one ▶
☐ author
☐ other copyright claimant
☐ owner of exclusive right(s)
☐ authorized agent of ____________
Name of author or other copyright claimant, or owner of exclusive right(s) ▲
of the work identified in this application and that the statements made by me in this application are correct to the best of my knowledge.

Typed or printed name and date ▼ If this is a published work, this date must be the same as or later than the date of publication given in space 3.

date ▶

Handwritten signature (X) ▼

11

MAIL CERTIFICATE TO

Name ▼

Number Street Apartment Number ▼

City State ZIP ▼

Certificate will be mailed in window envelope

Have you:
- Completed all necessary spaces?
- Signed your application in space 10?
- Enclosed check or money order for $10 payable to *Register of Copyrights*?
- Enclosed your deposit material with the application and fee?

MAIL TO: Register of Copyrights, Library of Congress, Washington, D.C. 20559

* 17 U.S.C. § 506(e): Any person who knowingly makes a false representation of a material fact in the application for copyright registration provided for by section 409, or in any written statement filed in connection with the application, shall be fined not more than $2,500.

☆U.S. GOVERNMENT PRINTING OFFICE: 1981: 355-305 Nov. 1981-135,000

Figure 4.2: Reverse of Copyright Form TX

- Works consisting entirely of information that is common property and containing no original authorship. For example: standard calendars, height and weight charts, tape measures and rules, and lists or tables taken from public documents or other common sources.

How long copyright protection lasts

Works originally copyrighted on or after Jan. 1, 1978. A work that is created (fixed in tangible form for the first time) on or after Jan. 1, 1978, is automatically protected from the moment of its creation, and is ordinarily given a term enduring for the author's life, plus an additional 50 years after the author's death. In the case of "a joint work prepared by two or more authors who did not work for hire," the term lasts for 50 years after the death of the last surviving author. For works made for hire, and for anonymous and pseudonymous works (unless the author's identity is revealed in Copyright Office records), the duration of copyright will be 75 years from publication or 100 years from creation, whichever is shorter.

Works that were created before the new law came into effect, but had neither been published or registered for copyright before Jan. 1, 1978, have been automatically brought under the statute and are now given federal copyright protection. The duration of copyright in these works will generally be computed in the same way as for new works: the life-plus-50 or 75/100-year terms will apply to them as well. However, all works in this category are guaranteed at least 25 years of statutory protection.

Works copyrighted before Jan. 1, 1978. Under the law in effect before 1978, copyright was secured either on the date a work was published, or on the date of registration if the work was registered in unpublished form. In either case, the copyright endured for a first term of 28 years from the date it was secured. During the last (28th) year of the first term, the copyright was eligible for renewal. The new copyright law has extended the renewal term from 28 to 47 years for copyrights that were subsisting on Jan. 1, 1978. However, the copyright must be timely renewed to receive the 47-year period of added protection.

For more detailed information on the copyright term, write to the Copyright Office and request Circulars R15a and R15t. For information on how to search the Copyright Office records concerning the copyright status of a work, ask for Circular R22.

International copyright protection

There is no such thing as an "international copyright" that will automatically protect an author's writings throughout the entire world.

Protection against unauthorized use in a particular country depends, basically, on the national laws of that country. However, most countries do offer protection to foreign works under certain conditions, and these conditions have been greatly simplified by international copyright treaties and conventions. Almost all developed free countries in Europe, North America and Asia are part of this convention. For a list of countries which maintain copyright relations with the United States, write to the Copyright Office and ask for Circular R38a.

The United States is a member of the Universal Copyright Convention (the UCC), which came into force in 1955. Generally, a work by a national or resident of a country that is a member of the UCC, or a work first published in a UCC country, may claim protection under the UCC. If the work bears the notice of copyright in the form and position specified by the UCC, this notice will satisfy and substitute for any other formal conditions a UCC member country would otherwise impose to secure copyright. A UCC notice should consist of the symbol © accompanied by the name of the copyright owner and the year of first publication of the work.

If you, as an author, want protection for your work in a particular country, you should first find out the extent of protection of foreign works in that country. If possible, this should be done before the work is published anywhere, since protection may often depend on the facts existing at the time of first publication.

If the country in which protection is sought is a party to one of the international copyright conventions, the work may generally be protected by complying with the conditions of the convention. Even if the work cannot be brought under an international convention, protection under the specific provisions of the country's national laws may still be possible. Some countries, however, offer little or no copyright protection for foreign works.

Who may file an application form?

The following persons are legally entitled to submit an application form:

- The author. This is either the person who actually created the work, or, if the work was made for hire, the employer or other person for whom the work was prepared.

- The copyright claimant. The copyright claimant is defined in Copyright Office regulations as either the author of the work or a person or organization that has obtained ownership of all the rights under the copyright initially belonging to the author. This category includes a person or organization who has obtained by contract the right to claim legal title to the copyright in an application for copyright registration.

- The owner of exclusive right(s). Under the new law, any of the exclusive rights that go to make up a copyright and any subdivision of them can be transferred and owned separately, even though the transfer may be limited in time or place of effect. The term "copyright owner" with respect to any one of the exclusive rights contained in a copyright refers to the owner of that particular right. Any owner of an exlusive right may apply for registration of a claim in the work.

- The duly authorized agent of such author, other copyright claimant, or owner of exlusive right(s). Any person authorized to act on behalf of the author, other copyright claimant or owner of exlusive right(s) may apply for registration.

Application forms

There is no requirement that applications be prepared or filed by an attorney.

For original registration

Form TX: for published and unpublished non-dramatic literary works.

Form PA: for published and unpublished works of the performing arts (musical and dramatic works, pantomimes and choreographic works, motion pictures and other audiovisual works).

Form VA: for published and unpublished works of the visual arts (pictorial, graphic and sculptural works).

Form S: for published and unpublished sound recordings.

For renewal registration

Form RE: for claims to renew copyright in works copyrighted under the old law.

For corrections and amplifications

Form CA: for supplementary registration to correct or amplify information given in the Copyright Office record of an earlier registration.

Other forms for special purposes

Form GR/CP: an application to be used for registration of a group of contributions to periodicals in addition to an application Form TX, PA or VA.

Form IS: request for an import statement under the manufacturing provisions of the Copyright Act.

For more information about all these forms, write for Circular R1c.

Application forms are supplied by the Copyright Office free of charge. Photocopies of application forms are not acceptable for registration.

You may order application forms at any time by telephoning 202/287-9100. Your order will be recorded automatically.

How to secure a copyright

Under the new law, copyright is secured automatically when the work is created — in effect, your book is copyrighted as soon as you write it. Registration is not necessary, it is not a condition of copyright protection. But there are advantages.

For example, registration establishes a public record of the copyright claim and is often necessary before any infringement suits may be filed in court.

Notice of copyright

When your book is published, a notice of copyright should be placed on all publically distributed copies. This notice is required even on works published outside the United States. Failure to comply with the notice requirement can result in the loss of some rights you would otherwise have.

The use of the copyright notice is your responsibility and does not require advance permission from, or registration with, the Copyright Office.

Form of notice

The copyright notice should contain the following three elements:

1. The symbol ©, or the word "Copyright" or the abbreviation "Copr."

2. The year of first publication of the work. In the case of compilations or derivative works incorporating previously published material, the year of first publication of the compilation is sufficient.

3. The name of the owner of the copyright (probably your name), or an abbreviation by which the name can be recognized, or a generally known alternative designation of the owner.

Example: ©1981 John Doe.

In general, if you do not print the copyright notice on your book, or you make an error in the name or date, you are still protected — provided you registered your book before or within five years after the publication. Also, once you discover the omission or mistake, you must make a reasonable effort to add the notice to all copies later distributed in the United States.

Registration procedures

In general, if you choose to register your work, send the following three elements to the Copyright Office in the same envelope or package:

1. A completed application form.

2. A $10 fee for each application. Do not send cash — use a check, money order or bank draft payable to the Register of Copyrights. Attach it to the application securely.

3. A deposit of the work being registered. The deposit requirements vary according to the situation, but the general requirements are:

- If the work is unpublished, one complete copy.

- If the work was first published in the United States on or after Jan. 1, 1978, two complete copies of the best edition.

- If the work was first published in the United States before Jan. 1, 1978, two complete copies of the work as first published.

- If the work was first published outside the United States, whenever published, one complete copy of the work as first published.

Complete the application form using ink pen or typewriter. All material and communications sent to the Copyright Office should be addressed to the Register of Copyrights, Library of Congress, Washington, D.C. 20559.

For printed information put out by the Copyright Office, or for answers to special questions relating to copyright problems, write: Information and Publications Section, LM-455, Copyright Office, Library of Congress, Washington, D.C. 20559.

Remember that the Copyright Office is not a lawyer's office — it is not permitted to give legal advice. So if you need guidance on matters such as disputes over the ownership of a copyright, or if you think someone has copied your book without your permission, it may be necessary to consult an attorney.

5

Using Words To Create Your Riches

You will learn in this chapter how to put together a successful book. Follow the steps I have outlined, the same steps I and other successful authors take, and you could have a best seller on your hands. I enjoy excellent book sales and so can you — just follow my steps.

Choosing Your Topic

Big publishers look for topics with mass audience appeal to meet and justify huge production and promotion costs, but, as a self-publisher, you are not so restricted.

Topics successfully exploited by self-publishers fall into two categories:

1. Those of general interest to a large, easy-to-reach audience, for example: books on human relationships, fitness and general health care, pop psychology, moneymaking and personal finance, etc.
2. Those of special interest likely to appeal to only a narrow audience, for example: books on Mongolian cooking, wood-burning stoves, Early American quilts, pre-War German coins, waste disposal systems, white-water canoeing, handwriting analysis, etc.

Note that neither category includes fiction or poetry. Some poets and authors are successful self-publishers, and they have a flare for writing, for characterization and plot, for making the abstract concrete.

Poetry and fiction have the highest failure rate of any type of book. Writing poetry or fiction is not easy. As the famed New York Times columnist, Red Smith, once noted: "There's nothing to writing. All you do is sit down at the typewriter and open a vein."

So, be warned: The self-publisher generally does better selecting a likely audience and concentrating on supplying the buyers with specialized non-fiction information.

Virtually anyone who can think clearly and has a rudimentary knowledge of grammar can write non-fiction. You don't have to be Hemingway. Writing form isn't that important — content is. People buy self-instruction books not for their literary style, but for the know-how and information they convey.

However, if you don't feel you can manage the project, if you lack the desire to write or simply the time, there are profitable alternatives explained in the next chapter.

Here are a few titles that give you an idea of the wide variety of marketable topics, the first section appealing to a massive market, the second to a specialized one.

Massive:

I Can If I Want To, Your Erroneous Zones, Never Cooked Before Cookbook, Decorating, How To Prosper During the Coming Bad Years, How to Get Out of Debt, How to Fall Out of Love, Dress For Success and *I Haven't a Thing to Wear.*

Special-interest:

The Old-Fashioned Recipe Book, The Whole Earth Catalogue, How to Keep Your Volkswagen Alive, Professional's Guide to Public Relations Services, The Zucchini Cookbook and *Postal History of Spain.*

If you know a lot about a subject — perhaps you've rebuilt the engine of your VW Bug four times — it is a natural topic for your book. If you think you don't know enough about any particular subject or issue, choose one that has always interested you.

Of course, you can always tailor your subject so that it appeals to the desires of a wide audience. Let me help by showing you what people want.

People want:

- To be in better shape and have the chance of a longer life.

- To have more comfort and luxuries.
- To have more money.
- To be more popular and attractive.
- To have more leisure time.
- To have security for their old age.
- To get praise.
- To save time.
- To be good parents.
- To be fashionable.
- To be influential.
- To have fun.

And there are hundreds of topics under the "how-to" category: *How to Win Contests, How to Borrow Money, How to Collect Stamps for Profit, How to Be Healthy and Live Longer, How to Move House, How to Write Classified Ads, How to Design and Write Display Ads, How to Improve Your Personality, How to Get Raises and Promotions, How to Play the Guitar, How to Become a Fund Raiser, How to Make Money With Your Camera, How to Hypnotize, How to Buy and Sell Antiques* — the list is endless.

Whatever your topic, the next step is in the direction of your local library, do to research.

Research

Remember, the librarian is your friend, and the library is perhaps your most valuable tool. Use all the libraries in your area — employees of public, city and county, community college and university libraries are more than pleased to help researchers. It's their job and they probably enjoy it.

Look through the library's title index file for titles of books dealing with your chosen topic that the library carries or can obtain for you from libraries in other cities.

Also, check a copy of *Books in Print* — it lists all books still in print by subject, author and title. Perhaps the library has some of them; others you can order from the publisher or browse through or buy at your local bookstore.

Often, by the time a book gets to print, its information is out of date or the methods it advocates have been improved. Magazines usually provide the latest information available on any given topic, so look through the *Reader's Guide to Periodical Literature,* which lists magazine articles on thousands of subjects and tells in which issue the article was printed. If you can't figure out how this essential magazine system works, ask your librarian.

Magazine articles also supply you with the names of experts in the field you are writing about — call or write them for information; if they live near, request a face-to-face interview. They, in turn, will know other experts and can lead you to other information sources.

In addition, look up the *Encyclopedia of Associations,* or write for a copy to Gale Research Company, Book Tower, Detroit, MI 48226. Information on virtually any topic can be got through this listing of almost 15,000 reference centers and organizations. Also, the free *Gale Research Company Cataglog,* available from the above address, lists a variety of reference books on numerous subjects.

Some of the material and information you collect will come from copyrighted pieces, so if you use large sections of the work word for word, ask permission and acknowledge the author. Most authors are delighted if you use their work in your book. It gives them added exposure and prestige. In fact, you'll notice that many of the exhibits in this book come from other books.

The key to the copyright law, which prevents the author's work from being used for profit by others without his permission, is that it protects only the order of printed words, not the ideas expressed. If you express another person's ideas in your own words or relay the same information using different words, you should be OK. A rule of thumb is to make sure you don't copy from another's work more than three or four words in a row.

Gather far more information than you will use — you will throw out the excess baggage as you write and end up traveling light.

Outline: Initial Organization

By now, you will have a pretty good idea of what you want to say, so figure out the logical order in which to say it. If describing a step-by-step or chronological process, the order is obvious; if not, one order — perhaps dealing with increasingly complex instructions —

will be better than all others.

Write up a table of contents, listing chapters in order and the information to be covered in each; then collect all your notes and research, assemblying them in separate piles for each chapter.

Writing

If you have a word processor, all the better, but a typewriter is fine.

Go through your research for the first chapter and organize that in a logical order. Type out the information, but don't worry about perfection on the first draft — just get it down on paper. You will have ample opportunity to correct, add and delete.

No one can teach you style or how to write, but there are guidelines:

1. Use short, strong Anglo-Saxon words, rather than those of Latin origin; i.e., use "gut," not "intestine."

2. Avoid fancy words. Most people use fewer than 800 of the 26,000 available words in the English language, and so should your book. Remember: You are trying to communicate, not impress.

3. Use nouns and verbs that express action; avoid superlatives and use adjectives and adverbs sparingly.

4. Show rather than tell. Use words that allow the reader to "see" what you are saying by describing the response of the five senses. The reader can paint a mental picture if you introduce touch, taste, sound, smell and sight.

5. Use lively quotes and humorous stories and examples to illustrate your points.

6. Organize paragraphs. Each paragraph is like a chapter — it must have a clear beginning, middle and end. The first sentence of a paragraph (the topic sentence) should both state the subject of the paragraph and link it to the preceding paragraph (a transition). The final sentence should link the paragraph to the next.

7. Write naturally. Write like you speak, using words and phrases that come readily to you. Pretend you're writing to a friend.

8. Relax.

Chapter by Chapter

Finish the first draft on each subject and chapter one at a time — this will help you concentrate and organize your thoughts.

When a chapter is finished, proof-read and edit it, cutting out repetition, rephrasing awkward sentences and, if necessary, reorganizing the material.

Professional Help

It is difficult for an author to edit his own work, so get a friend or pay an editor to read through your material.

For a list of ghostwriters, freelance writers and editors, contact Research Associates International, 340 E. 52nd St. New York, NY 10022. Also, see the *Writer's Digest Yearbook,* which lists some available writers. If you have a hard time finding someone you feel will do a very good but inexpensive job editing your book, consider hiring an English or journalism major at a university or junior college near you. You won't have to pay a student much for quality work, provided you hire the right person. Place an ad in your local college newspaper.

Once your book has been edited at least twice, type the final version on paper or on a word processor disc.

Choosing a Title

A good title will boost book sales drastically. Some catchy, highly successful titles that have become standard phrases are: *I'm OK, You're OK, The One Minute Manager, Your Erroneous Zones, Zen and the Art of Motorcyle Maintenance, Catch-22* and *Real Men Don't Eat Quiche.* There are hundreds more.

A good title arouses curiosity, plays on words, is titilating and prompts people to buy the book. A dull title will hurt your sales and probably damn your book to failure. Here is a tried-and-true method that will help you select a good title.

1. Look in the chapter on advertising under the section on headlines. A good headline for an ad will usually be a good title for your book. After all, they both serve the same purpose of enticing a person into reading further.

2. Make sure your title is aimed at your specific audience. If you are selling a book on a money-raising program for those looking to make money, why not call it *How To Use Your Hidden Potential To*

Get Rich? Notice how the title arouses curiosity.

3. Use easy-to-understand words. If you use very sophisticated words, potential customers will think you are looking down on them. And if they think that, they won't buy your book.

4. Gain credibility by listing specific information in your title. A good example is the title of this book. I could have called it, *Making A Fortune In Mail Order;* instead, I used a specific amount of money ($500,000) and a specific amount of time (one year).

No matter what title you choose, test it. Ask your friends what they think. I write out a list of titles I like and then ask my friends to pick the one they prefer. Ask why your friends chose the title they did — this gives you insight into what people like and will buy. The better the title, the more dollars in your pocket.

6

Alternatives To Writing

You may find, after struggling over your typewriter for a few hours or a few days, that writing is not for you, that you don't have the time or the inclination. If so, don't worry; there are alternatives.

Ghostwriters

Hiring a ghostwriter is a good idea if you don't feel you have the time or talent to write your book. But just because you hire someone else to write it doesn't mean you can hoist all the responsibility for your book on to the ghostwriter. Remember, it's still your book.

You will have to write an outline of your book, detailing what information you want in what chapters. If you are an expert on your subject, work closely with your ghostwriter — tell him where to research, relay to him information and experiences that only you, as an expert, know.

In addition, while the book is being written, look over the ghostwriter's shoulders — make sure he writes what you want and is not going off on tangents. But you must recognise the fact that your ghostwriter is a professional and probably knows what he is doing. Listen to his suggestions.

Last but not least, make sure the writer you hire is good. Read carefully some of the books or articles he has written. Make sure he has the type of style and personality you want, because they will be reflected in your book. If he is a negative person, your book will have negative overtones. If the writer is arrogant, your book will seem arrogant to the reader. Be concerned about this — it may make the difference between a best seller and a flop.

For available ghostwriters and advice on how to pick one, see the "Professional Help" section in the previous chapter.

If you consider this option, remember that it is the most expensive open to you.

Wholesale books

You will have to buy books for at least 70% off the original cover price to make a good profit selling wholesale books by mail order. Often, books offered wholesale are good books that were badly promoted.

There are several companies that sell many, many titles at wholesale or discounted prices. You might try these:

American Book Dealers Exchange, P.O. Box 2525, La Mesa, CA 92041.

Premier Distributing Co., 16254 Wedgwood, Fort Worth, TX 76133.
They offer free catalogs listing hundreds of titles for $1 and more in many general-reference categories. Drop-ship and dealer discounts.

Argus Communications, 7440 N. Natchez Ave., Niles, IL 60648.
Offers several popular inspirational books, some in color, for about $5 to $15. Dealer discounts.

Outlet Book Co., Inc., One Park Ave., New York, NY 10016.
Offers nearly 6,000 reference and educational books on history, life stories, crafts, general information and religion. Dealer discounts of 40% to 70% off list price.

Johnson Smith & Co., 35075 Automation Dr., Mt. Clemens, MI 48043.
Offers a variety of books and pamphlets on home entertainment and hobbies. Prices are 12 books for $5, retailing at $1 each; 12 books for $10, retailing at $2 each; or 100 books for $70, retailing at $2 each.

Arco Publishing Co., 219 Park Ave., So., New York, NY 10003
Offers hundreds of books on a wide variety of topics.

How to slim down.
Save energy. Care for your car.
Complain effectively. Heat with wood.
Remove a stain. Check for breast cancer.
Select a smoke detector. Help kids to study.
Control pests. Cope with arthritis. Get a patent.
Insulate your home. Control your blood pressure.
Buy an IRA. Get rid of a headache. Spot a con job.
Keep records. Invest. Make toys out of junk.
Budget your money. Repair a leaky faucet
Prevent drug abuse. Pay for an education.
Garden organically. Restore an old house.
Start a small business.
Learn the metric system.
Jog successfully. Buy land.
Read labels. Avoid sunburn.
Relieve the common cold.
Eat better. Save money.
Administer first aid.
Reduce cholesterol.
Find a job. Retire.
Tune up your car.
Grow tomatoes.

No matter what kinds of questions you have, there's a good chance the Consumer Information Catalog can help you find the answers.

Inside, it lists more than two hundred federal publications you can send for on all kinds of subjects. All contain a wealth of information.

Really helpful information.

The catalog was put together by the Consumer Information Center of the U.S. General Services Administration. It's free. And so are many of the publications in it.

Now the only question left is how to get a copy.

Simple. Just write to:

Consumer Information Center, Department MN, Pueblo, Colorado 81009.

GSA A public service message from the U.S. General Services Administration · Consumer Information Center

Figure 6.1: Free government publications

Wilshire Book Co., 12015 Sherman Rd., North Hollywood, CA 91605
Offers more than 400 titles of self-improvement books.

Lion Publishing Co. P.O. Box 151034, San Diego, CA 92115
Offers a variety of self-improvement and mail order titles.

Remainder books

Remainder books are a real bargain. In some cases you can buy them for less than the cost of printing them.

Remainder books are books that usually didn't sell well and the publisher is trying to unload them. If it costs a publisher $1 to print a book and you buy it for 50 cents, you have a good remainder deal. But there is a catch — you may have to buy several thousand copies.

Remainder books can require a heavy investment and, while the book may have been poorly promoted, it is probably out of print for good reason.

Several companies offer remainder books, as well as promotions, closeouts and overstocked titles of every conceivable type, up to 90% off their original list prices. If you are interested, contact these companies:

Crown Publishers, One Park Ave., New York, NY 10016.
Discount Reader's Service, 1060 Twin Silo Lane, Huntington Valley, PA 19006.
Overstock Book Co., 120 Secatogue Ave., Farmingdale, NY 11735.
Overstock Bookseller, 30-2 Chambers, Danbury, CT 06810.
Publishers Books, P.O. Box 1140, Clearwater, FL 33517.
Publishers Central Bureau, One Champion Ave., Avenel, NJ 17131.
Tartan Book Sales, P.O. Box 921, Williamsport, PA 17701.
Worldwide Book Service, 251 Third Ave., New York, NY 10010.

Books with expired copyrights

The old copyright law gave a book 28 years of protection before the copyright expired. If you can get a book that is older than 28 years and its copyright hasn't been renewed, you can reprint it with no royalty fee. If you get a book that is older than 56 years, it is usually in the public domain. Books in the public domain belong to the general public, and you have every right to reproduce them.

To sell books with expired copyrights, you must first reproduce them, which can cost you lots of money. Unless you can finance reproducing these books and you know for sure they will sell, don't undertake this venture. Don't forget that few books that old have material that is applicable and useful to readers in the 1980s.

The biggest advantage you will get from books in the public domain is the ability to copy pictures, paragraphs and quotes for inclusion in your own book.

Contact the Copyright Office at: Register of Copyrights, Library of Congress, Washington, DC 20559, for information on the copyright status of a particular book.

Government publications

The U.S. government is the biggest publishing house in the world, and anything it puts out is public property and is in the public domain, so you can use, copy and reproduce it at will. You can reproduce any government publication or book in its entirety, or you can just pick out interesting bits of information. However, you can't just reproduce a government publication and sell it for profit.

Some people use government publications for the research portion of their book. The amount of material you can glean from the government and the many studies its agencies conduct is amazing, and you should take full advantage of it.

If you would like to receive government publications that are of interest to consumers, write Consumer Information, Pueblo, CO 81009 and ask for the free catalog. Many of the publications are free and the rest can be purchased at cost.

Books with reproduction rights

Some of you may not have the time, skills or money to write your own books. What do you do then? Lion Publishing Company offers a *Self-Publisher's Opportunity Kit,* available for those who are serious about making money selling books by mail.

The kit contains eight interesting books — they've all been tested and are proven sellers with a large audience. Each book comes with a copyright agreement that allows you to reprint and sell as many copies as you desire.

You can then reprint each book for as little as 50 cents each at your local printer.

The self-publishing kit comes with complete step-by-step instructions on how to market these books for the greatest profit. You will also receive a very effective sales letter that will move your books immediately. In addition to the sales letter and books, you get proven-effective classified ads to use to promote your books. These classifieds employ the best sales techniques available.

You can choose to combine two or more of the titles to create a completely different book, or you can sell each book just as it is. The books are yours to do with as you will.

Here is a brief description of each of the eight books in the *Self-Publisher's Opportunity Kit.*

1. How to Get Free Grants

Do you know that the government and foundations give out billions of dollars in free grants every year? Some of this could be yours, easily — all you have to know is how to get it, and that's what this book is all about. The book tells you which institutions will give you money and how best to apply for the grant so that you are sure to get it.

Some highlights of *How to Get Free Grants* are:

- How to get a $150,000 grant for being a woman in business.
- How to get up to $3 million in grants if you are a minority in business.
- How to get your foot in the door for corporation grant money that must be given away.
- How to get some of the billions of dollars given away each year by corporations seeking tax deductions and write-offs.
- A complete list of U.S. government departments that award grants.
- Government organizations that help low-income people get financial help.
- A detailed collection of 200 private foundations that await your grant application.
- How to have the government send you money every year to pay for your education.
- How to get cash grants of $1,800 just for having a low income and for going to college.

- Complete, step-by-step methods of applying for free grants: how to fill out the application, write the letter of appeal, and other support data.

All this money awaits you — it can be yours, just for the asking. Won't you stake your share?

2. Importing — Your Key to Success

Do you know that you can buy virtually any product made in the United States for much less money abroad? There is a great profit potential in importing from countries all over the world. If you enjoy traveling, this a great way to deduct all your vacations as well as making a profit by going overseas.

Highlights of *Importing — Your Key to Success,* include:

- Details of products you can bring into this country and pay no duty.

- U.S. Customs Service loopholes to use when shipping products into this country.

- A complete list of more than 200 companies that will drop-ship mail order products to you.

- How to receive FREE products from almost any manufacturer, just for asking for them.

- How to determine if the product you choose will make you a fortune.

- How to travel FREE, with the foreign manufacturers of products paying your way to their countries.

- A list of FREE publications from countries all over the world.

- How to make millions in commissions for locating suitable products for interested firms.

- How to use all the importing tax breaks to reduce your taxes.

- How to get government agencies to help you import your product.

This guide is more than a book, it is a complete manual to importing success. Use it to create an importing empire.

3. Success on the Job

Do you have the job you want? Or are you overworked and underpaid? This book will help you in your search for "job happiness." Learn how to apply for a job and be hired as the top candidate. Move up the ladder of job success with ease. Win over your supervisors and fellow employees. Impress your boss so much that he gives you bonuses and raises. Moving up in a company can be so simple and rewarding. The secret is knowing what to do.

Some highlights of *Success On The Job* are:

- How to get that interview with ease at the company of your choice.
- What you should and shouldn't say at the interview.
- How to win your superiors over to your way of thinking.
- How to get what you want at work with the unique "assertiveness training" method.
- How to increase your productivity on the job while working less.
- How to be liked and admired by your superviors and coworkers.
- Many methods on how to get a raise and promotion in no time at all.
- How to prepare persuasive and result-getting resumes.

Getting ahead on the job has never been easier. This book can show you how to make more money while working — working smarter, not harder.

4. Making a Fortune with Real Estate

Millionaires are created every day with real estate. You, too, can make big money in real estate with "no money down." This manual tells you how to spot instant moneymaking investments. Isn't it about time you got your share of the real estate profits?

Highlights of *Making a Fortune with Real Estate* are:

- How to spot foreclosure bargains, sometimes at 20% of their market value.
- How to buy real estate with no money down, then sell the property to make an instant profit with no investment.
- How to get the best financing possible with creative financing techniques.
- Geographical areas that give you the greatest return on your investment.
- How to spot property that sells for half its true market value.
- How to use other people's money for your investments.
- How to reduce your tax bill to almost nothing with real estate investing.
- How to triple your initial investments within a year.
- How to get low-interest government financing just for the asking.
- How to create a positive cash flow with the real estate you buy.
- Where to find rural land bargains you can get for 10 cents on the dollar.
- How to buy land at a fraction of its cost at tax auctions.

It is a myth that you need money to buy real estate. Anyone with no money and the right instructions can become a millionaire through real estate acquisition. Start accumulating thousands of dollars of real estate with this book.

5. The Secret of Raising Money

Getting a loan can be hard, or it can be very easy. If you do the right things to the right person, you have a much better chance of success. I not only show you how to get that extra money you need, but also how to clean up a bad credit history and how to get the lowest-interest loans possible. Do you know that you are eligible for government-subsidized, low-interest loans? These and many other available sources of money are yours, waiting only for you to apply for them.

Some of the highlights of *The Secret of Raising Money* are:

- How to borrow $50,000 on your signature, for any purpose.
- How to wipe out your debts without bankruptcy.
- How to raise $200,000 in 24 hours with no collateral.
- An 11-step method that turns bad credit ratings into AAA-1 ratings.
- How to buy valuable apartments, homes and land for next to nothing at government auctions.
- How to take over on-going businesses with zero cash.
- Government agencies that will lend you up to $150,000.
- How to get up to $1 million from private investors for your investment project.
- Setting yourself up as a $100,000-a-year money broker.
- How to get free food, car, rent, medical care and travel expenses.
- How to avoid paying taxes forever, legally, with this proven, eight-step plan.

Getting the right loan is a matter of proper timing and know-how. This book teaches you both. Learn the techniques for getting low-interest money.

6. The Millionaire's Secret of Growing Rich

Millionaires make 10 to 100 times what you make, but they aren't 10 to 100 times smarter than you. What do they do that you don't? They use the full ability of their minds. Imagine what you could do if you used the same systems they use to make themselves wealthy. You can with this informative, wealth-building book.

Some highlights of *The Millionaire's Secret of Growing Rich* are:

- Exposing your hidden talents with "self-evaluative psychology" and put them to good use making money for you.

- How to unlock your potential to make you millions.

- A five-step procurement process that will get you virtually anything you want.

- The art of making complicated decisions in five easy steps.

- Effective time management, which allows you to do twice as much in half the time.

- How to solve any problem with the Downy seven-step problem-solving schedule.

- How to turn the negative aspects in your life into profitable opportunties with "adversity reversal" techniques.

- "Networking," and how it can get you to the top.

Millionaires use systems to make money. To do the same, all you need are those systems, and this book has them all.

7. How to Influence People and Win Them Over

This book will show you how to understand and get along with people so that they enjoy and desire your company. After using the influencing techniques, you will find that people feel good around you — you will understand their needs and fulfill your own. Winning others over to your way of thinking has never been easier.

Some highlights of *How To Influence People And Win Them Over* are:

- "Transcendental" influencing skills that make it easy for you to influence others.

- How to get maximum self-disclosure from others after perfecting the art of listening and talking.

- How to apply "projection analyzation" used by psychiatrists to win over defensive people.

- How to persuade others to give you what you want by using "assertion techniques."

- Thirteen systems that get people to like you.

- "Criticism-reversal" techniques to get the better of overly critical people.

- How to use the five-step "self-promotion" method to get people to know you quickly.

- How to analyze people correctly and understand their needs.

The ability to get along with all people is priceless. Winning people over has become a science, and this book gives you the step-by-step instructions you need to master the art of being liked by other people. It's easy to understand and apply.

8. How to Get $200,000 in Benefits from the U.S. Government

We all pay taxes — but how many of us get all the money from the government that we should? Very few. A recent survey shows that the average American receives only 11.8% of the money for which he or she is eligible. Do you get your share?

A few highlights of *How to Get $200,000 in Benefits from the U.S. Government* are:

- How to get up to $67,500 from HUD to buy a condominium.

- How to get up to $5,000 a year for your education, as long as you make less than $20,000 a year.

- How to get a guaranteed $50,000 loan if you live in a rural area and would like to improve living conditions.

- How to get a direct loan of up to $25,000 to search for minerals.

- How to get a guaranteed loan of up to $1.5 million for your fishing vessel.

- Details on low-interest business loans of up to $500,000.

- How to buy U.S. government surplus equipment and supplies for 10 cents on the dollar.

- How to win oil and gas leases at government-held public auctions.

- How to buy land through the U.S. Department of Land Management for as little as $10 an acre.

- How to secure $92,000 for home improvements.

The government set up these programs for all of us, but few people take advantage of these priceless opportunites, mostly because of lack of information. This book tells you about hundreds of programs and how you can get what the government owes you.

How to use your kit

You will receive by return mail the complete *Self-Publisher's Opportunity Kit* which includes eight professionally prepared books. In addition, you receive reprint rights that allow you to sell as many books as you like for as long as you like.

Each book is 8½-by-11 inches and is made to be easily reproduced. Take the books to your local printer and have them printed for about 50 cents a copy.

Everything you need is in your kit. Use the sales letter and the classified ads to sell your books. Special instructions are included so that you will know what to do every step of the way.

Here is what you receive

Eight well-prepared books written by leading authors, all specialists in their fields. None of these books can be bought in any bookstore. The eight books are yours to reprint and resell as many times as you want. They are:

1. How to get Free Grants
2. Importing — Your Key to Success
3. Success on the Job
4. Making a Fortune with Real Estate
5. The Secret of Raising Money
6. The Millionaire's Secret of Growing Rich
7. How to Influence People and Win Them Over
8. How to Get $200,000 in Benefits from the U.S. Government

A certificate entitling you to full reprinting rights for any or all of the eight books.

A complete set of instructions that shows you how to sell your books for the most profit. Directions on how to handle all types of publishing situations are also included.

A well-written sales letter that should get you good results. Classified ads for you to use are also included.

You will also receive a guarantee with your *Self-Publisher's Opportunity Kit.* If, for any reason, you are not satisfied with your kit, return it within 30 days for a full, unconditional refund.

The *Self-Publisher's Opportunity Kit* with eight books, certificate of reprint rights, step-by-step instructions, sales letter and classified ads, is only $25. Send all orders to:

Lion Publishing Company
P.O. Box 151034, San Diego, CA 92115

7

Saving Thousands On Printing

Before the computer, the invention of the printing press did more to revolutionalize society than anything else. It allows your words to reach thousands of people, and, in turn, to make you thousands of dollars.

Along with the process of printing your book come many exciting business and design decisions: Is this printer's work really up to my standards? What style typeface should I use? How should I design the book cover? You face dozens of exciting decisions. Let's go over them.

The Type

The first decision you must make is whether you want your manuscript typeset professionally or by you on your typewriter; both options have advantages and disadvantages. The do-it-yourself option will save you money but won't look as professional.

Let's discuss the do-it-yourself option first.

You'll need either a typewriter, a word processor or a computer with word-processing capabilities.

The typewriter

Using this option, you type your manuscript, double-spaced, on

Properties sold at a tax sale may be anything from vacant or developed land to apartment houses and industrial buildings. Properties almost always sell for much less than their true market values. Frequently, the minimum price accepted for a property is only a few dollars above the amount owed for back taxes. In some cases, people have bought $40,000. homes for less than $1,000., and $150,000. apartment houses for only $7,500. in back taxes.

Figure 7.1: Typewriter type

standard 8½-by-11-inch typing paper and deliver it to your printer. Don't worry that typewriter type can look tacky when used in books — it will look professional when reduced in size (usually at no charge) by your printer.

Your printer will then photograph and reduce your typed, camera-ready pages.

If you decide to type your book on a typewriter, it is best to use one with proportional spacing. On most typewriters, each letter takes up the same amount of space; but on a proportional-space typewriter, each letter takes up an amount of space proportional to its size. For example, the letter "i" takes up less space than a "p," which takes up less space than a "w." They cost more but the results look better.

You may want to have the lines of type in your book justified. This means making the right-hand margin a straight, vertical line, with all lines of type ending at the same point, like the lines in this book. Some typewriters come with right margin justification.

Alternately, you may want the lines of type "ragged." This means that the line ends at the end of a word, without hyphenation or justification, no matter where the word happens to finish. The right-hand margin is not a straight vertical line, but a "ragged" line. Choose whichever you like, although justified copy is the norm.

Ideally, your machine will be a proportional-space typewriter capable of self-correction and justification; several new models do it all. Brother puts out one of the least expensive, priced about $300 — shop around.

The copy you take to the printer should be error-free. Each page should be sprayed with a fixative immediately after it is typed to prevent smearing. Also, you should use a carbon-cartridge ribbon for crisp letters.

The word processor

Problems of proportional spacing, correction and justification disappear when you use a word processor. You can pick one up that will meet all your word-processing and financial-planning needs for about $1,000. With computer prices dropping the way they are, a computer may be within your budget. You'll have to shop around for this price and may have to pay extra for the printer and screen.

The key to getting a computer that meets your word-processing needs is to buy one that includes the software. They are not hard to find. One of the best word-processor programs available is *Wordstar,* a powerful program for editing a book. This program has one drawback — it can't do proportional spacing. For complete information, contact you local computer dealer.

Of course, an alternative to buying is renting. Expect to pay about $100 a month to rent a suitable computer.

Text written and printed on a word processor is, like typewritten or typeset pages, camera-ready. This means it is ready for the printer to photograph.

Money-saving tip: If you write your book on a word processor and want it professionally typeset, do not deliver a printed manuscript to your typesetter. Instead, deliver the computer discs on which your book is stored. These can be converted to the format your typesetter uses. His photocomposition machine can then set type directly from the disc. This means the typesetter does not have to retype and proofread your manuscript, saving time and your money. Giving the typesetter your floppy discs will cut your typesetting costs in half.

Another way to cut your typsetting costs in half by using a computer is to send your copy over the phone lines. How? With the use of a modem. A modem allows one computer to talk to another via the telephone. A modem will cost you about $300, so, if you are not going to use it often, don't consider it. The process is simple. Consult your local typesetter if you are interested.

If you do not have a word processor and want your work typeset, you can type the manuscript on a typewriter, rent a word processor, and transfer your manuscript onto floppy discs. Then deliver these floppy discs to your typsetter.

Professional typesetting

There are many different typestyles to choose from, but they all fall into three general categories: serif, sans serif and fancy. I recommend that you have your book printed in serif or sans serif typestyles

— stay away from the fancy. Fancy typestyles are attractive but hard to read. Your book should be easily read.

In the diagram are some of the more common typestyles. Notice the difference between serif and sans serif type. The serif letters have little ticks, or serifs, at the top and bottom; the sans serif letters do not, "sans" meaning "without" in French. This book is typed in sans serif. What type should you use for your book? It's a matter of your personal taste. I can tell you that traditional, conservative books tend to use serif, while liberal, modern books use sans serif.

There are hundreds of typefaces to choose from, but be careful — only a few are easily read and will fit the subject of your book. Your best bet is to pick a typestyle that is easily read and is commonly used. Consult your typsetter about the typestyles he has available because he can probably offer only a limited selection.

Here are some printing terms you will have to use:

Typeface: Standard and easy-to-read typefaces are English Times, sans serif Oracle and Baskerville.

Type size: A standard type size for books is 10-point. In printers' jargon, "points" measure the size of a typeface, the distance from the top of the letter "b" to the bottom of the letter "q." There are 72 points to the inch.

Leading: Two points leading is standard. Leading refers to the space between lines of type.

Unless you are trying to be unusually creative, which is, afterall, one of the advantages of publishing your own book, the following standard text will probably do: English Times typeface in 10-point letter size with two points of leading.

Of course, if you are typesetting your book yourself, your choice of typestyle is limited to that of your typewriter. However, you can vary the size of your typewriter type by having your printer reduce or enlarge your typed pages.

Headline Typestyles

Headlines are used to grab the reader, to entice him into the following body of copy. They should be larger than the type used for

Sample Typestyles

SERIF:

This is an example of English Times a serif typestyle that is easy to read and stylish without being too ornate.

This is an example of English Times Italic. Italic type is generally used to set something apart from the rest of the text such as the title of a book or newspaper.

This is an example of English Times Bold. Bold type is generally used when you want to call attention to an important point or idea.

SANS SERIF:

This is an example of Oracle. Oracle is the typestyle in which the text of this book is set. Oracle is a good choice when you don't want a typestyle that is too fancy or too plain.

This is an example of Oracle Italic. Italic type is generally used to set something apart from the rest of the text such as the title of a book or newspaper.

This is an example of Oracle Bold. Bold type is generally used when you want to call attention to an important point or idea.

FANCY:

This is an example of Commercial Script. Commercial Script is known as a "true" script typeface because the letters connect to one another like handwriting.

Figure 7.2: Sample typefaces

Type Size

This is 6 point type: Now is the time for all good men to come to the aid of their countries. Now is the time for all

This is 7 point type: Now is the time for all good men to come to the aid of their countries. Now is

This is 8 point type: Now is the time for all good men to come to the aid of their

This is 9 point type: Now is the time for all good men to come to the aid of

This is 10 point type: Now is the time for all good men to come to the

This is 11 point type: Now is the time for all good men to come to

This is 12 point type: Now is the time for all good men to

This is 14 point type: Now is the time for all good

This is 18 point type: Now is the time for

This is 24 point type: Now is

This is 30 point type:

This is 36 point type:

This is 12 point type with 1 point leading
This is 12 point type with 1 point leading

This is 12 point type with 2 points leading
This is 12 point type with 2 points leading

This is 12 point type with 3 points leading
This is 12 point type with 3 points leading

Figure 7.3: Sample type sizes and leading

the main body of work, but not so large as to be overpowering or threatening.

Again, you have a wide selection of styles to choose from and, if possible, your choice should reflect your subject matter. For example, a producer of crude oil or baseball bats would use a bold, strong style, while a seller of lace curtains or nylon stockings would pick a delicate, perhaps italic, style. This is even more of a consideration when choosing the style for the headlines on the cover of your book, and I'll discuss that later.

A simple rule of thumb is to use the same style for your headlines that you use for your main body of copy. This way, you use a standard typeface and indicate importance by varying the type size.

If your body copy is 10-point, use, for example, 36-point type for chapter numbers, 30 to 24-point for chapter heads and 18 to 14-point for subheads.

Choosing Your Typesetter

Expect to pay $7 per 5½-by-8-inch page for a professional to typeset your typed manuscript; if the type is set directly from a word processor disc, the charge will be nearer $3 a page. Remember that one typed page does not equal one typeset page — 100 typed, single-spaced pages equals about 70 typeset pages of equal size.

The typesetter you hire should have good references, samples of his work for you to examine and, above all, he should take pride in his task. Make sure the typesetter's previous work meets your standards.

Before you hand over any money, make sure you know the payment schedule, who will pay for errors and that all specifications (type and headline size, spacing, etc.) are clearly understood.

There are three typical payment schedules:

1. Half on delivery to the typesetter and half after final corrections have been made.

2. A third up front, a third on delivery and a third after final corrections.

3. Full payment only after the entire job is done.

Avoid a typesetter who wants full payment in advance.

Make sure the typesetter agrees to produce the first typeset copy at no charge so you can proofread it for errors. This final copy will be your last chance to make relatively inexpensive corrections.

If you do the proofing, make sure you have a firm grasp of English and its grammar; if you don't, hire a proofreader. Nothing is more tacky and unprofessional than a book with spelling and grammar errors, and you'd be surprised to know how many crop up in self-published works.

Return the proofread copy to your typesetter so he can make the necessary corrections; his next copy will be the final version, the camera-ready version that goes to the printer.

Every time you re-read and edit your manuscript, you will probably see errors or find a sentence you want to re-word. Remember that the farther along you are in production, the more costly the change is to make. Corrections on your second typeset version will cost about $1 each, or $40 an hour.

If you have a hard time locating a good, reliable typesetter, I can help you. All my typsetting, including this book, is done by Typecast Graphics, which sells its typesetting service by mail to mail order businesses. For a complete set of available typestyles and prices, write or call: Phil Green, Typecast Graphics, 5261 Tipton Street, San Diego, CA 92115, 619/286-6614.

Printing

Some mail order business dealers print their own books, and, although they save money on printing costs, there are disadvantages. First, presses are usually large and require a lot of space and initial capital. Second, unless your are an expert, the end result may look far from professional, so you should be willing to pay for professional know-how. Third, the time spent printing may be better spent on promotion, sales and your next book. The really successful mail order business people spend little time on the mechanics of production; rather, they concentrate on the mechanics of selling.

The qualities you should seek in a printer are price, quality and location.

Price: Get at least three estimates. Here is an example of what you might have to pay. For a manuscript delivered to the printer camera-ready, expect to pay between $8 to $10 a page for 500 copies of a 5½-by-8½-inch book on 50-pound white paper. You will get a price break if you print your book in multiples of 8 or 16. Consult your web press printer before deciding how many pages to include in your book.

Quality: Choose a printer who has obvious pride in his work, who is a stickler for details and perfection. Your customers will notice any mistakes your printer makes. You may have to pay extra for a quality printer, but it is worth it in the long run.

Location: The nearer the printer is to you, the better you are able to oversee the quality of your job.

Paper

There are two main types of paper you can use for your book. The first is newsprint, used for newspapers. The second is 50 lb. book stock. This type of paper is commonly found in books, such as this one. Generally, the "heavier" the paper, the better and more expensive.

Should you decide to use newsprint to save money, use ultrabright newsprint. It is whiter and brighter than that found in your daily newspaper and will make your book appear of higher quality. It costs more, but the extra cost is well worth it.

Types of Printing

There are two ways to print your book: web press printing and offset printing.

Web press

Web press printing is cheaper if you want to print in quantity, say more than 2,500 books. The press used is similar to a newspaper press, and is very quick and economical if you can justify a long run of books. If you choose web press printing, it is probably best that its cover be a "self-cover." This means that the cover of your book is of the same paper as the inside pages. Because web press printing with newsprint is relatively so inexpensive, placing a cover on the book may double the total cost. The web press printing can be arranged through your local newspaper printer. Look under "Newspapers" or "Web Press Printers" in the Yellow Pages.

For a 48-page book printed in ultrabright newsprint with a two-color self-cover, expect to pay about 26 cents a book for about 5,000 copies. One company that produces small books on a web press is Diner and Klein, founded in 1948. Their prices are good. Write for their free price list to, Dinner & Klein, 600 S. Spokane St., P.O. Box 3814M, Seatle, WA 98124.

Offset

In offset printing, a book is printed page by page. Your local printer, rather than newspaper, specializes in offset. It's relatively inexpensive for small runs but too expensive for long runs.

If you opt for offset printing, shop around for the best deal and for a printer who has pride in his work. Beware of middlemen who have no printing facilities — all they do is send your work to a printer and tack on an extra 20%.

The Printing Process

Let me tell you what process your offset printer goes through to create your books.

First, he will print your book on 8½-by-11-inch pages. Each one of these pages will actually be four pages of your 8½-by-5½-inch book. He then collates these printed pages either with a collating machine or manually; either way, he will charge you about 1 cent a page for collating. (A web press collates automatically.) He folds each page and puts two staples in the binding of the book to hold it together, then trims three edges of the book with his cutter. One of the reasons offset printing is more expensive than web printing is because much more manual labor is required.

If you would like a price quote for offset printing, look up "Printers" in the Yellow Pages; shop around.

For your book to have much chance of being displayed in bookstores, it will probably have to be web press printed. The cost is not prohibitive: For a 200-page, bound, 20 lb. book stock with a three-color, glossy, card-stock cover in a 5,000 book run, expect to pay about $1.15 per copy.

Having your book printed in 20 lb book stock and bound with a glossy cover is the quickest way to impress your market. Most publishers, including me, have their books printed this way. The book you are holding is hard bound, and cost me twice as much to print as a paperback edition would have. This book cost about $2.30 each in a 5,000 book run.

The Cover

Your book can be hardcover or paperback. The most expensive books are those with a hardcover and a dust jacket such as the one you are holding. A dust jacket protects the book as well as sells it. Many libraries prefer the hard-bound edition of a book, because it has a longer "shelf life," but some are starting to buy paperback books to cut costs. Let me point out that a book with a hard cover will cost from $1 to $2 more per book (in a 5,000 book run) than a paperback. In other words, it costs about twice as much to print a hard-bound book than a paperback, all other factors being equal.

A paperback cover should be 10 to 12 point C1S, a measure of the thickness of the cover stock. You must choose between varnishing your cover or laminating it with plastic, which will make the cover last much longer but cost you more. However, for a quality paperback, you will have to laminate the cover and pay the extra cost. If a printer can do lamination in-house, it won't cost that much more.

8

All About Art

Artwork — photographs, line drawings, graphs — can greatly enhance the written word, as well as break up large chunks of printed type and make the whole package more attractive. They also add to the cost, so you will have to decide what you want and what you can afford.

If you feel confident and you are good at art, do the art work yourself; if not, hire a professional artist. The only problem with hiring an artist is the cost — anywhere from $20 to $40 an hour.

Artists create what are called line drawings, which have the advantage over photographs of bringing out more details. I'll show you how you can get inexpensive line drawings even if you are not a good artist, but let me first discuss photographs.

Photographs

You can always use a photograph instead of hiring an artist to draw a picture. They are, afterall, cheaper. Make sure you can take good pictures — an amaturish picture will cheapen your book. You can hire a professional photographer, but shop around for the best price. Perhaps one of your friends who is a good photographer has a

Figure 8.1: 100-line-screen halftone

David Bendah
Figure 8.2: Enlarged halftone

Figure 8.3: 55, 85 and 100-line-screen

35mm camera and can develop and print black-and-white film.

All photographs you use must be converted into halftones. A halftone is a photograph of your photograph made up of hundreds of little black dots. The little dots make it possible for the press to print the pictures. Before you convert your picture into a halftone, you must know how many dots per line you want. I have included a picture converted into 20, 40, 60, 80 and 100 dots per line.

A screened picture is a picture converted into halftones or dots. Be warned that not all presses can print screens of more than 100 dots per line.

Inexpensive Art

There are alternatives to hiring an artist to do your pictures. One is called "clip art" — ready-made black-and-white line drawings you can use in your books with no danger of infringing copyrights.

I once wrote a book on horse race handicapping and needed pictures of horses running. So I bought a clip art book on sporting events that had three pages of galloping horses which were perfect for my book. The clip-art book cost me only $10, a far better deal than paying an artist at least $300 for the same result.

Figure 8.4: Clip art

You can buy ready-made clip art that fits your needs perfectly at your local art store. If not, try *The Mail Order Clip-Art Handbook.* It specializes in mail order illustrations and headlines for all kinds of mail order products; it also has headlines you can use in mail order ads. The book is 8½-by-11 inches and has 60 pages of clip art. If you can't find it at your local art store, I will send you a copy postpaid for $15. Just write Lion Publishing Company.

Free Art

Here is another way to save money on illustrations. Art work more than 50 years old is usually in the public domain, meaning that no one has rights to it and that it is free for anyone to use. Your public library probably has old art books containing art in the public domain; look also in old magazines and newspapers.

You can obtain a complete catalog of books that contain outdated art from Dover Publications, 180 Varick St., New York, NY 10014. Write them for details.

Layout

It is important to lay out your book correctly and with style. You want the design to interest your readers, to enhance their interest in your book. Buy paste-up paper at a local art store. It makes a good guideline for positioning your pages. You will need a light table — you can make your own by putting a lamp under a piece of glass. If you have your book printed, make sure to use a 70 lb paper stock so that your paste-up sheets hold up.

Number the pages at the bottom or top of the page. Notice that I put my name on the right hand side of every page. This is so that you will remember it. You need camera-ready copy so that your printer can print your book. Figure 8.6 is a typical ad layout, so use it as a guideline to paste up your full-page ad.

Camera-Ready Copy

Camera-ready copy is pure black or red ink on white paper. In most cases, the printer can shoot the copy even if the paper is colored. Check with your printer. Light blues are invisible to the printer's camera. You can use a light blue pen or marker to write on your copy — it will not show up when your copy is printed. You can purchase this type of pen at your nearest art shop. Do not erase on

Figure 8.5: Picture in public domain (1909)

the original copy. You can use liquid paper to cover dirt, smudges and anything you don't want to show up on the printed page. Leave a ¼-inch margin on all four sides of anything to be printed — this allows the printing press to grab the paper and leaves room for trimming the book.

You need a knife to cut your paper. The best is an exacto knife, which costs about $1. You also need a substance to stick your paper on your paste-up grids. You have a choice of rubber cement or Lectro stick wax. The reason I mention only these glues is because they don't shrink and allow you to reposition your paper if you are not happy with how you set it. Rubber cement is an inexpensive alternative. It goes on easily but is rather messy. It also turns brown after three years. Another option is a waxer with wax. A waxer (about $45) rolls sticky wax on your paper. You then position your paper. The wax is clean, always stays sticky and is easy to use. If you do a lot of paste up, my advice is to get a waxer — you will save a lot of time and money. If you don't do that much, rubber cement is fine.

As I said earlier, you must convert all your photographs into halftones, copies of your photograph that are made up of many small dots. If you look at a picture printed in a newspaper through a magnifying glass, you can see the dots easily. It costs about $5 to have a halftone done. You can have them done cheaper on a copy machine, but the quality won't be as good. Have your printer or your typesetter create all your halftones.

The camera will pick up only what it sees. If you have copy that is very difficult to clean up, and you don't want it retypeset, don't worry — there is an easy solution. Have a "stat" made of the copy, and then clean up the stat. A stat is a picture of your copy. Your typesetter or printer can produce a stat for you. Remember the fundamental rule of printing: "A clean and neat original will produce clean and neat copies."

Make sure all your pages are stuck on straight. If they aren't, they will print crooked. I use a light table; others use T-squares or drafting machines. The most inexpensive way to align your pages in with a T-square. Use light blue grided paper. The grids are light blue so that the camera can't see them. You can buy this paper at your local art store. Using a light table is probably the easiest way to paste up your book. A light table will cost you anywhere from $100 to $200.

Cover Design

There is an old saying that you can't tell a book by its cover; that

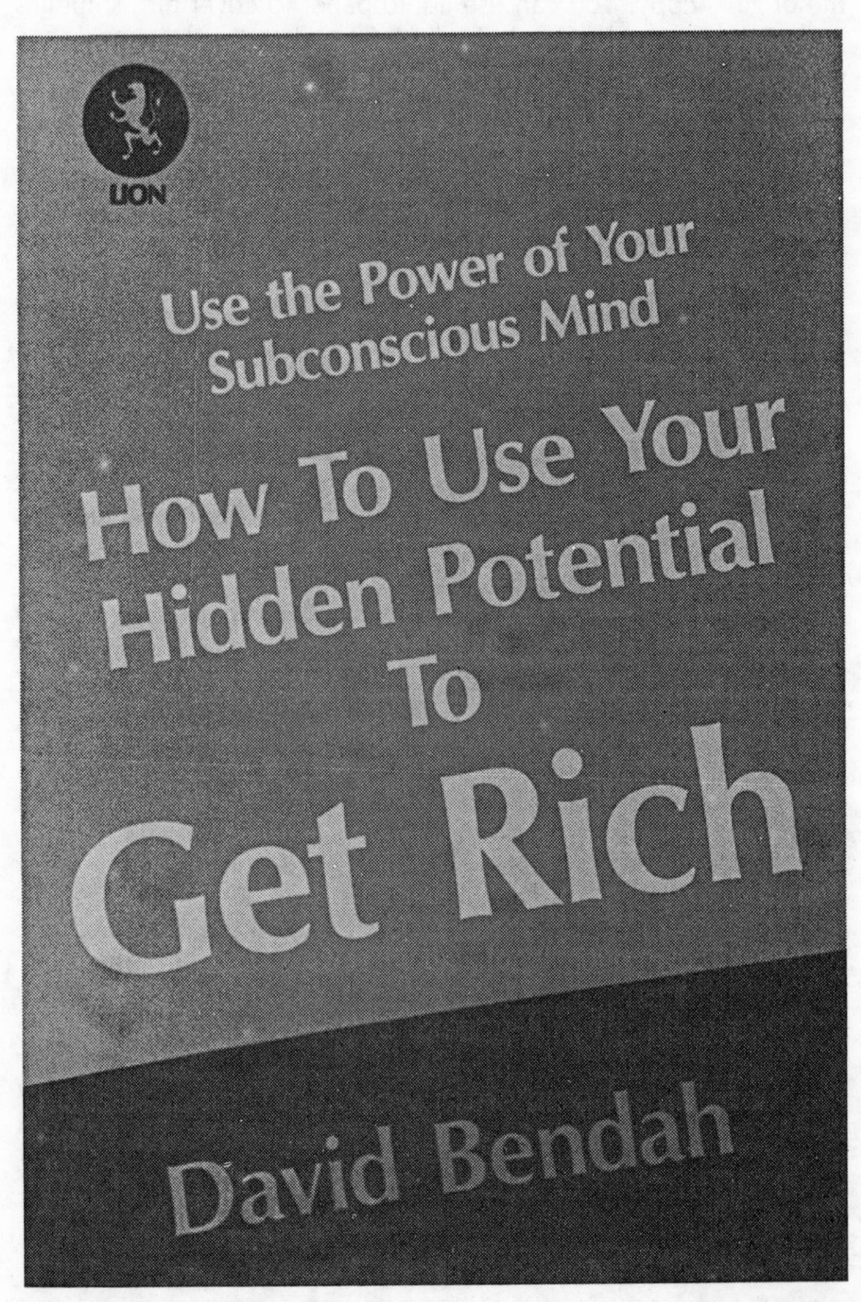

Figure 8.6: Front cover of How To Use Your Hidden Potential To Get Rich

How To Use Your Hidden Potential To Get Rich

By David Bendah

Outline of Contents

1. Tapping Into Your Hidden Potential
2. The Power Is Within You
3. How To Get What You Want
4. Making Your Dreams Come To Life
5. Using Your Hidden Computer To Solve Complicated Problems
6. Securing Your Goals
7. The Super-Influencing Technique
8. How To Gain Happiness
9. How To Achieve Perfect Relationships
10. Creating The Successful You
11. The Secret Of Making Your Mind Work For You
12. Using Persistence To Get What You Want
13. How Others Will Lead You To Success
14. Knowledge: The Key To Success
15. Your Ultimate Doctor
16. Your Road To Success

About the Author

David Bendah has written numerous books on using the subconscious mind to better yourself. He delivers speeches and conducts workshops on training and using the hidden powers within you. Thousands of people have attended his activities. His books and seminars have given birth to a new breed of successful people all over this nation. He is one of the foremost authorities on using the mind to its full potential.

If you would like to attend one of his activities or would like David Bendah to speak at one of your functions, please contact him at P.O. Box 151034, San Diego, CA 92115.

Figure 8.7: Back cover of How To use Your Hidden Potential To Get Rich

may be true, but you can certainly *sell* a book by its cover. Other than your advertising, the cover is perhaps the most important selling tool you have once the book reaches bookstores. If done right, the cover catches the eye of a would-be book-buyer, distinguishing your book from the hundreds surrounding it on bookstore shelves. It also draws the buyer into the contents and persuades him to take the book home.

Remember: Color sells. Spend the extra money for color. At the very least, use two strongly-contrasting colors (one of them could be red because, studies show, that color attracts and sells best). If possible, use a photograph or illustration, but don't let it detract from the actual title of your book.

Make sure you use a good bold sans serif or slight serif type that is easy to read. Don't be overly creative with your cover. If you are, people may not be able to read its title. You want to shout the title of the book at potential customers. Using subtitles is optional. Your name, as author, should go at the top or bottom of the cover. Any testimonials you may have will be helpful.

I know you have already made sure that you have a catchy title on your book. Let me show you what else you can do to the cover to make it stand out. Look at the cover of this book. Notice that the most important things on the cover are, "$500,000" and "Mail Order." Notice that they are larger than the rest of the title of the book. The same is true for the cover of my other book, *How To Use Your Hidden Potential To Get Rich.* The most import words — "Get Rich" — are the largest; next in size are "Hidden Potential." "How to Use Your" are the smallest.

It is customary to put your name on the bottom of the book, in smaller type than the title, unless you are a well-known author. If you make your name too large people will think you are egotistical.

The back of your book can have a paragraph entitled "About The Author," that tells about you and your qualifications. You can also have a picture of yourself. The back cover could also contain points of interest or chapter headings. I have displayed the back of one of my books.

There are disadvantages to printing a price on your cover — what if you decide to raise or lower your price? I discuss this in detail in Chapter 9.

The spine of your book should contain the title of your book, the author's name and the name of the publishing company. If you have your book printed in newsprint on a web press, you won't have to worry about what goes on the spine because there is no spine.

Your ISBN

The ISBN, in use since the '60s, is an international book identification system that helps prevent errors in ordering and shipping. Every edition of every book should have an ISBN, which greatly aids the distribution of books, especially in this age of computer ordering and invoicing. Look at the bottom back cover of this book and you will see an ISBN number.

To get an ISBN (it's free), request a "Title Output Information Request Form" from the International Standard Book Numbering Agency, 205 East 42nd St., New York, NY 10017.

Because you may well write more than one book, ask the numbering service for 100 titles. You will be sent a card with your ISBN "publisher identifier" number and a sheet with space for 100 titles and editions. It's your job to give every new title an ISBN suffix.

A standard ISBN is 0-924723-78-2. The "0" means the book was published in an English-speaking country. The "924723" is the "publisher indentifier," which identifies the publisher. The "78," the suffix you must add yourself once you are started in the ISBN system, indentifies the title and edition. The "2" is a math function that ensures the other numbers have not been miscopied.

The ISBN should be printed in 12-point OCR-A type:

1. In the bottom right corner of the back cover and jacket.

2. On the top edge of the left-hand jacket flap.

The OCR-A type (optical character recognition) can be "read" by automatic cash registers. If your typesetter or printer does not have the proper typeface, rent the appropriate type ball for an electric typewriter and type it on yourself.

Your LC listing

Also on the copyright page should go your Library of Congress catalog card number. For your number, before your book is printed, write to Library of Congress, Washington, D.C. 20540 and ask for "Procedures for Securing Preassigned Library of Congress Catalog Card Numbers" and the "Request for Preassignment of LCC Numbers" application form 607-7.

SAMPLE OF COMPLETED FORM

FOR INTERNAL USE ONLY
PUB.
IMPR.

TITLE: Children's Wonderland of Toys
SERIES: Games & Toys Around the World, no. 3
Original Title, if any: --
Foreign Language: -- Translation ☐, from what language:

PUBLISHER: Kidsbooks
Address 100 Main Street
New York, NY 10000

AUTHOR(S): John Doe
DISTRIBUTOR, if other than publisher:
EDITOR(S): --
IMPRINT:
TRANSLATOR(S): --
Appendix ☐ Bibliography ☐ Footnotes ☐
Index ☐ Other:
ILLUSTRATOR(S): Mary Smith
Programmed Book ☐
INTRO. BY; PREFACE BY; etc. --
ILLUSTRATIONS (KIND & NUMBER): 19 color drawings
Reissue ☐ New Edition ☐ First U.S. Edition ☐
PAGES: 120
Import ☐, If yes, are you exclusive distributor?
AUDIENCE: Adult Layman ☐, (Also suitable for Young Adults? ☐)
Adult Professional ☐ College Text ☐
Simultaneous cloth & paper publication XX Talking Book ☐
Elhi Text ☐: Grade: Juvenile ☒: Grade: 3-5

BRIEF DESCRIPTION OF BOOK
A pictorial survey of toys popular with children in different parts of the world.

Original Paperback ☐
Revised ☐ Abridged ☐ 2nd Ed. ☐ Other
PUBLICATION DATE:
Reprint ☒: If reprint, name of orig. publisher & orig. pub. date
1965, (Building Blox Lib)

ENTER PRICE(S) BELOW:

		INT'L. STANDARD BOOK NUMBER
On short discount (20% or less) ☐		
HARDCOVER TRADE:	6.95	ISBN 0-1234-5678-X
If juv., is binding guaranteed?		
LIBRARY BINDING:	- -.- -	ISBN - - - - - - - - - -
HARDCOVER TEXT:	- -.- -	ISBN - - - - - - - - - -
PAPER TRADE:	4.95	ISBN 0-1234-4987-6
PAPER TEXT:	- -.- -	ISBN - - - - - - - - - -
TCHRS. ED.:	- -.- -	ISBN - - - - - - - - - -
WKBK:	- -.- -	ISBN - - - - - - - - - -
LAB MANUAL:	- -.- -	ISBN - - - - - - - - - -
OTHER: SPECIFY	18.95	ISBN 0-1234-4983-7

Software Diskette and Book Pkg.

AUTHOR/EDITOR/ILLUS. BIOGRAPHICAL INFORMATION
John Doe is currently a nursery school teacher in New York City.

ADVERTISING, PROMOTION & PUBLICITY PLANS
direct mail and Bowker bibliographies

SUBJECT CATEGORY: 167, 147

ISBN NOTE: If you assign your own ISBNs, put full 10 digit number in spaces above. The system requires a separate ISBN for each edition

LC #: 78-12345
Order # (optional): 987A
7
Completed by: John Q. Public

Figure 8.8: Page of Books in Print

Figure 8.9: Mark Danna and Dan Poynter's The Frisbee Player's Handbook

Whereas you have a different ISBN for each edition of your book, you have one LC number assigned to your work, whatever the edition.

Your UPC

You probably won't need a Universal Product Code at first, not until your book sells enough to warrant more than one edition or until it proves to have enough mass-audience appeal to be sold in supermarkets. The bar code, which is read by a machine, identifies the ISBN, the price, the publisher and the title.

Book Shape

Unless you hire out most of the work involved in producing your book, you will have to make several design decisions.

The further you deviate from the standard, the more your book will cost to produce. But, if you can afford it, you can give your artistic impulses full reign, making your book large, small or irregularly shaped.

For example, Mark Danna and Dan Poynter's *The Frisbee Player's Handbook* is shaped like a Frisbee and is packed in one of the famous flying discs. It was expensive to produce but an effective display item.

If cost is a major factor, use the size paper that printers are used to working with. For books, that's 5½-by-8½ inches or 8½-by-11 inches. Using standard sizes will save you money.

9

How To Cut Mailing Costs

You are in luck. The postal system subsidizes postage for mailing books. You can mail your books at a fraction of what you would have to pay to mail just about anything else. Because of these breaks, you can run your mail order business with a moderate postage bill.

The first step is to meet your local postmaster or talk with the postal clerks to learn what breaks are given small businesses; they are helpful and welcome new mail order firms.

You should also have a fair knowledge of the laws and regulations concerning use of the mails. Get a copy of the postal guide from the Superintendent of Documents, Government Printing Office, Washington, DC 20402.

Special Fourth-Class Book Rate

The post office offers a special fourth-class book rate: 69 cents for the first pound, 25 cents for every additional pound up to 7 pounds, and 15 cents each additional pound over 7 pounds. You must stamp "special fourth-class book rate" on each package.

Apart from the low cost, an advantage of this rate is that you don't have to meet various requirements of other cut-cost postal services. For example, you don't have to sort your mail into ZIP-code sequence; nor do you have to mail more than 200 pieces at a time or have a total weight of at least 50 pounds.

Books sent at this rate should reach their destination as quickly as packages sent bulk rate. You can use this low rate to mail books anywhere in the United States and Canada.

Other Special Book Rates

You should take advantage of special rates for shipping books out of the United States.

If you are shipping more than 15 pounds of books, you may qualify for the "Direct Sacks Of Prints" rate — only 55 cents a pound with a 15-pound minimum and 66-pound maximum. This rate is offered to encourage publishers to print their books in the United States, then export them to foreign markets. If publishers had to pay normal postage rates, they would have their books printed in the foreign country in which the book is to be sold.

Should you want to mail less than 15 pounds of books overseas, you must use a different rate. This rate, for international parcels of printed matter, is only for packages that weigh less than 5 kilograms, or 11 pounds. Packages weighing more than 5 kilograms must be broken down into lighter parcels.

You may qualify for a special library book rate if you are mailing books to libraries. The library rate is 40 cents for the first pound, 14 cents for each additional pound up to 7 pounds, and 84 cents for each pound over 7 pounds.

Bulk Mailing

Use the bulk rate if mailing more than 200 pieces or if the total weight of your mailing is at least 50 pounds. To use this rate, every piece must be the same size and you must sort the packages according to ZIP code.

Mailing bulk is one of the cheapest methods of advertising your book. If you have at least 200 identical sales pieces to mail, each weighing less than 3.4948 ounces, you qualify for the piece rate. The rate is 12.5 cents per piece.

If each of your mailing pieces weighs more than 3.4948 ounces and the total weighs more than 50 pounds, you may use the pound rate: 38 cents per pound and 4.2 cents per piece.

You must sort your mail by ZIP code, which is the main reason the post office offers you this low rate. Sorting your own mail isn't that hard and the time you spend is well worth the money you save. If you are buying a mailing list, ask the seller to arrange the names in

ZIP-code sequence.

Pieces qualifying for the rate must be sorted in the sequence shown in the self-explanatory diagram.

All bundles should have more than 10 pieces and should be less than 4 inches thick. A good thing about bulk mailing is that the post office supplies you with free mail sacks, rubber bands, mail forms and all the advice you need.

Bulk mailing imprints

For a bulk mailing, you need a bulk-mailing permit costing $50 a year. After you buy one, affix either a "bulk rate permit" imprint, a "bulk rate cancelled" stamp or a "postal meter imprint" stamp on each envelope to signify you have a bulk mail permit. The three methods you use to show you are doing a bulk mailing cost the same, but each has its advantages.

1. Bulk rate permit. A bulk rate permit is printed on each envelope by your printer. This saves a lot of time and money because you will not then have to affix postage on each letter. There is one disadvantage to this method: Some people throw away all mail with a bulk-mail imprint. I know I do. To many, the imprint is a sure-fire way of identifying junk mail.

2. Cancelled stamp. Pre-cancelled stamps best mimick 1st Class postage. These bulk rate stamps stick on to envelopes just like ordinary stamps, but they cost only 12.5 cents each. They are the hardest to affix to your letter but, because they appear to have been sent 1st Class, they get the greatest response.

3. Postal meter imprints. These also can be used to mimick 1st Class mail. To make the imprint on your envelopes, you need a Pitney Bows or other postage meter. The advantage of using this type of bulk mail imprint is that your potential customer will probably think the mail is important and open the letter. The drawbacks are that you must rent your postage meter for about $30 a month and must buy a bulk mail imprint slug for about $20. Make sure your meter can be set to divisions of a 1/2 cent because the bulk piece rate is 12.5 cents each letter. If your meter can't be set to 12.5 cents, you must pay 13 cents a letter.

Other Ways To Deal With Mailing Costs

- Get charts listing the latest postal rates from your post office. Use a scale to determine required postage. Regularly check your scale

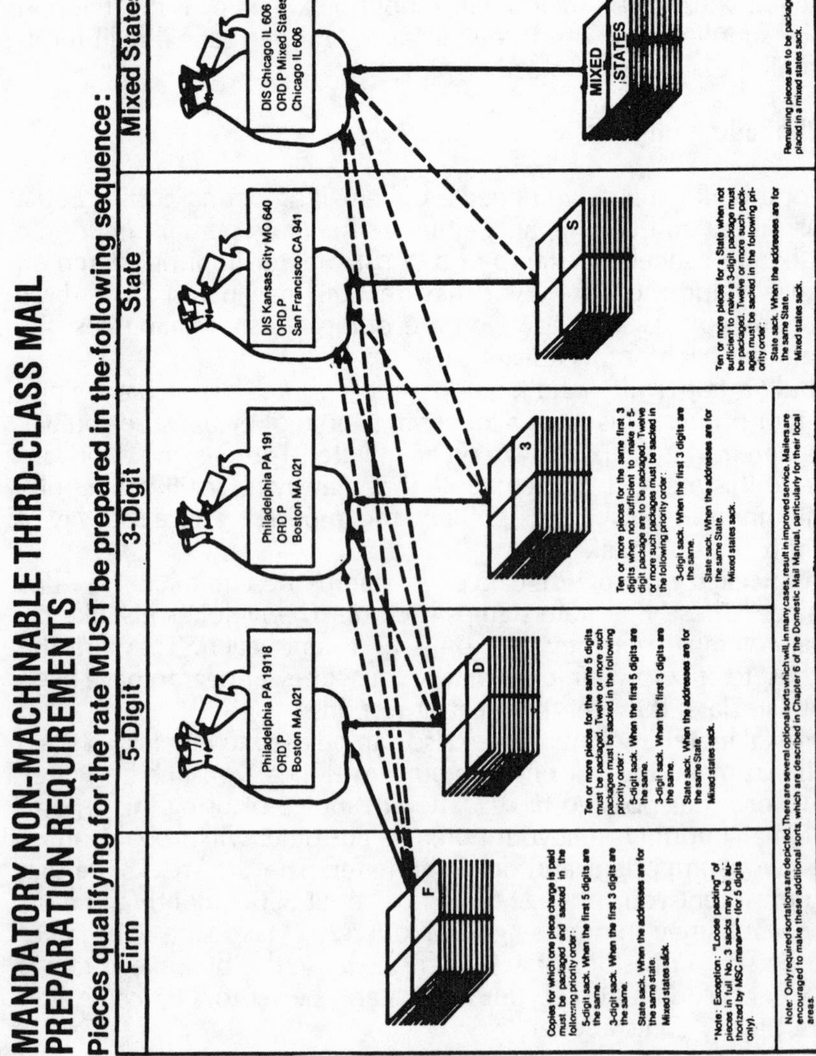

Figure 9.1: How to sort for a bulk mailing

145.5 Format of Permit Imprints. Permit imprints must be prepared in one of the following formats. Any of the formats may be used to display the information prescribed by 145.3. The addition of extraneous matter is not permitted.

a. **First-Class Mail**

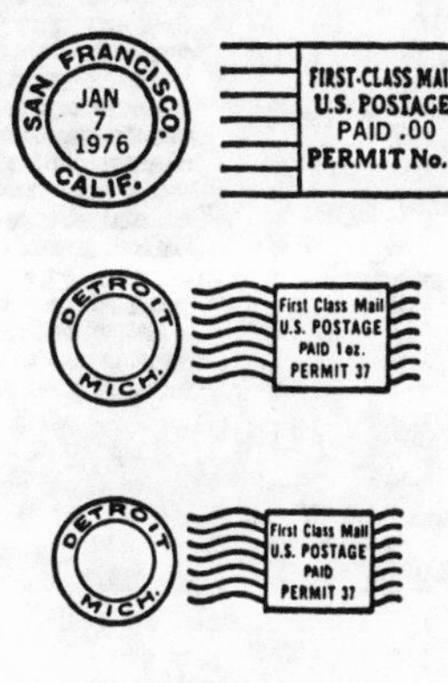

FIRST-CLASS MAIL
U.S. POSTAGE
PAID
New York, N.Y.
Permit No. 1

PRESORTED
FIRST CLASS MAIL
US POSTAGE PAID
NEW YORK, NY
Permit No. 1

b. **Second-, Third-, and Fourth-Class Mail *(Date and First-Class Mail Omitted)***

U.S. POSTAGE
PAID
New York, N.Y.
Permit No. 1
ZIP Code 10001

U.S. POSTAGE
PAID
New York, N.Y.
Permit No. 1
ZIP Code 10001

U.S. POSTAGE
PAID
John Doe Company

BOUND PRINTED MATTER BLK RT
US POSTAGE
PAID
New York, NY
Permit No. 1

FOURTH-CLASS BULK RATE
U.S. POSTAGE PAID
NEW YORK, NY
Permit No. 1

PRESORTED
SPECIAL FOURTH-CLASS RATE
US POSTAGE PAID
New York, NY
Permit No. 1

c. **Bulk Third-Class Mail**

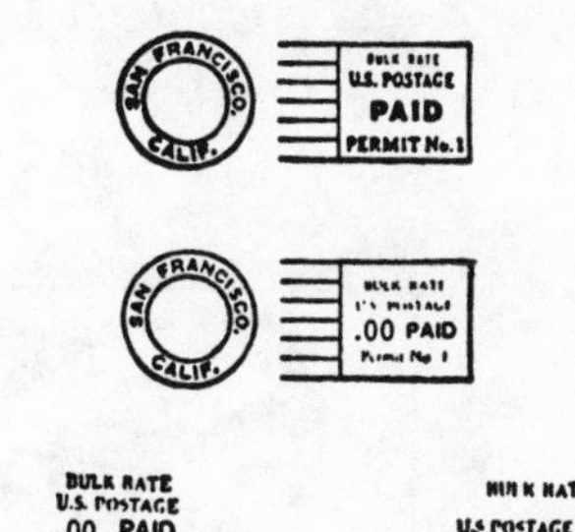

BULK RATE
U.S. POSTAGE
.00 PAID
Chicago, Ill. 60607
Permit No. 1

BULK RATE
U.S. POSTAGE PAID
John Doe Company

d. **Special Rates for Authorized Organizations Only**

Nonprofit Organization
U.S. POSTAGE
.00 PAID
New York, N.Y.
Permit No. 1

Figure 9.2: Bulk mail imprints

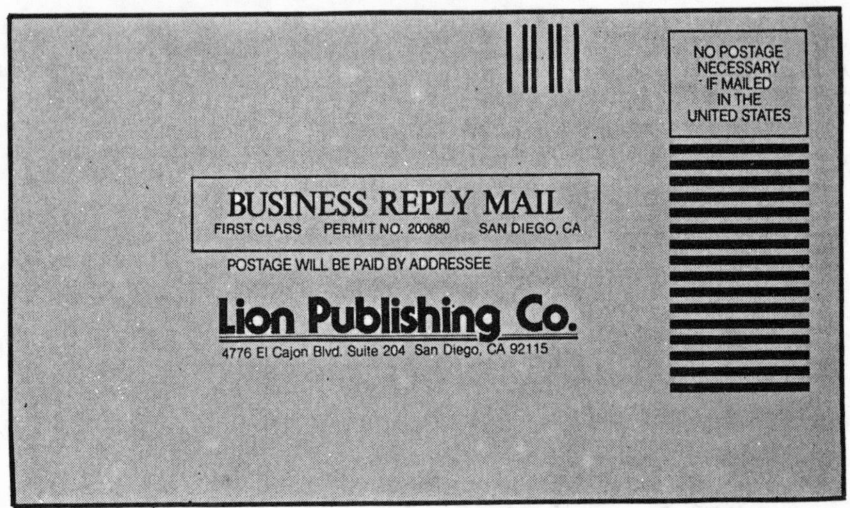

Figure 9.3: Return reply envelope

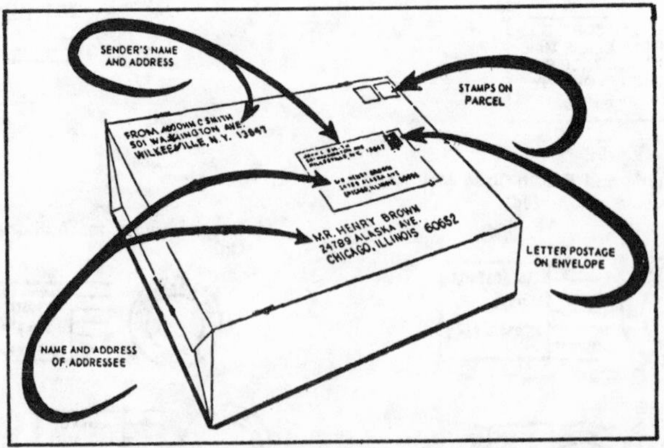

.24 Parcels which bear address labels shall have the regular or postage meter stamps affixed by accepting postal employees so that the stamps overlap the upper right corner of the label, as shown in the following illustration:

Figure 9.4: 1st Class letter affixed to parcel

for accuracy by weighing nine pennies — they should weigh 1 ounce.

- Pay companies, such as some mail order firms, to mail your circulars with theirs. They charge about 4 cents per circular to mail your piece to their customers.

- Pay "postage due" charges on in-coming mail — the envelope might contain a large order. You could write "refused" on a "postage due" package and send it back to your customer; but your customer, who may have made an honest mistake, will think that you are cheap and unwilling to spend a few pennies for his business, and may cancel his order.

- Think carefully about how you ask your customer to pay the cost of mailing his order to him. You can simply say in your ad, "Add 10% for postage." Occasionally, a customer will forget to add the extra payment, or will leave it off on purpose. When I get small orders without the postage payment, I just mail off the order and take the loss; if the order and postage cost is large, however, I send out the books with a nice reminder of the money due. Sometimes it works, sometimes it doesn't, but a slight loss is better than an angry customer and a canceled order.

- Another way of covering postage costs is to say, for example, "Send $10 plus 50 cents postage and handling," or, "Send $10.50, including postage." In both cases, the price to the customer is the same, but the second example sounds like a better deal — you are including something in the asking price instead of adding an extra charge.

Remember, use of the mails carries with it the requirement that you be honest at all times, and, in addition to the U.S. Postal Service, the Federal Trade Commission may keep tabs on you. The FTC investigates customer complaints about products and deceptive advertising. It also checks all media for doubtful advertising claims, and its investigations can lead to regulatory action. To make sure you meet every FTC requirement, get the FTC advertising standards from the Bureau of Anti-Deceptive Practices in Washington, D.C.

No matter how careful you are, you may unknowingly break a post office or FTC rule if you are given false information about the book you plan to sell. You should therefore have available good legal counsel

10

Book Basics

Pricing Your Book

The price of your book will have a drastic impact on its sales, so consider it carefully.

Most books and pamphlets sold though mail order cost between $2 and $20, but prices go higher. For example, the titles in one Durst Publications book list range in price from $2 for a pamphlet on counterfeiting to more than $40 for a dictionary of Greek coin inscriptions.

Big publishers try for a 500% markup, selling to retailers for five times the cost of the book to cover huge publishing and promotion costs. You, however, have different factors to consider.

When pricing your book, you must consider your time, production costs (typesetting and printing), and, often the greatest expense, advertising. You must also decide if you want to sell a large number of books quickly by making your book inexpensive, or if you want to get the highest price possible, even if it slows sales.

Printing a price on your book is not always a good idea. After your book is printed, you may find the price too low or too high. Also, as inflation is always with us, you can change your asking price merely by changing your ad. Not printing a price gives you price flexibility.

How Much Can You Get By Mail?

If your per-book cost is $1.25, a standard rule is to sell it to wholesale book dealers for $2.50, (double your costs), to retailers for $5 (four times your costs) and to mail order customers for $10 (eight to 15 times your cost). Mail order allows you to get the most money for your book because your potential customers haven't yet seen it and their curiosity will prompt them to pay more.

Here's an example of what two mail order book publishers are selling their books for.

The National American Institute put out a book by David Martin called *The Easy Path To Riches.* This 90-page book is about investing in real estate and sells for about $10. *The Crandall Secret,* by Daniel A. Crandall, is 178 pages — it, too, sells for $10. Believe me, none of these books would sell in a bookstore for their mail order price. To sell in bookstores, the prices would have to be cut at least in half. The price advantage is one reason mail order book selling is profitable and popular.

As a rule, you will not be able to charge eight times the cost of your book. You should charge what the market will bear. Sometimes it is more than eight times; other times it is less. You can get $20 for your 50-page book if it is what people really want to read about. You can also get $2 for your 50-page book if people already have similar material at home or if the market is flooded. If you want to know how high to price books, study similar books and price yours accordingly.

When Should I Sell?

If you were selling tennis rackets and snow shoes through the mail, you would have to consider what months these seasonal items sell and in what areas they're needed. Tennis rackets aren't much good when there's two feet of snow on the ground; snow shoes don't go over big in Hawaii.

But because you're selling books — popular items any time, anywhere — this is one mail order strategy you can ignore.

Figure 10.1: Mail order response rates, percentage expected for each day.

Day	%Response
Monday	31.7
Tuesday	8.4
Wednesday	9.6
Thursday	19.4
Friday	15.5
Saturday	16.0

Almost. It's well known among mail order business people that some months are better sellers than others, no matter what or where you sell. As a general rule, fewer sales are made in the summer months (June, July, August) than in the winter (December, January, February).

Here are charts of mail order results by day and by month. They will give you a good indication of when to sell.

Figure 10.2: Mail order response results by month (base: January = 100).

Month	%Rating
January	100.00
February	97.3
March	83.7
April	74.1
May	72.5
June	68.7
July	75.2
August	81.7
September	85.0
October	88.3
November	80.8
December	72.1

When Should I Send?

When should you send? You should send NOW. Promptness in filling your orders ranks right up there with price and product quality in traits a mail order business should exibit.

Promptness is not only good business practice, it is required by Federal Trade Commission regulations.

Of course, there will be times when you are unable to fill an order quickly — if you're ill, out of stock or out of town. But that doesn't relieve you of the responsibility of acknowledging the order. Under the FTC ruling, you must fill orders within 30 days. If you cannot, you must notify your customer of the delay, explain it, give a possible delivery date and offer a full refund. If you don't, and the customer complains to the FTC, you may face regulatory action.

If a customer orders a book which you are out of and don't plan on restocking, you can do one of two things: return his money, an unpopular ploy with most mail order businesses; or credit the amount to his account, a much more popular move because the customer usually orders additional merchandise.

If you are unable to fulfill this obligation, it is your responsibility to get someone else to do it for you. So, too, is it your job to make sure your drop-shipper, if you are using the drop-ship method, delivers orders promptly. If he doesn't, you get the complaints and you should find a replacement.

Apart from obeying regulations, promptness also enhances your reputation and increases the chance of repeat orders. Of course, some customers will be beligerent over the slighest delay — which

Figure 10.3: Paid circulation sales chart

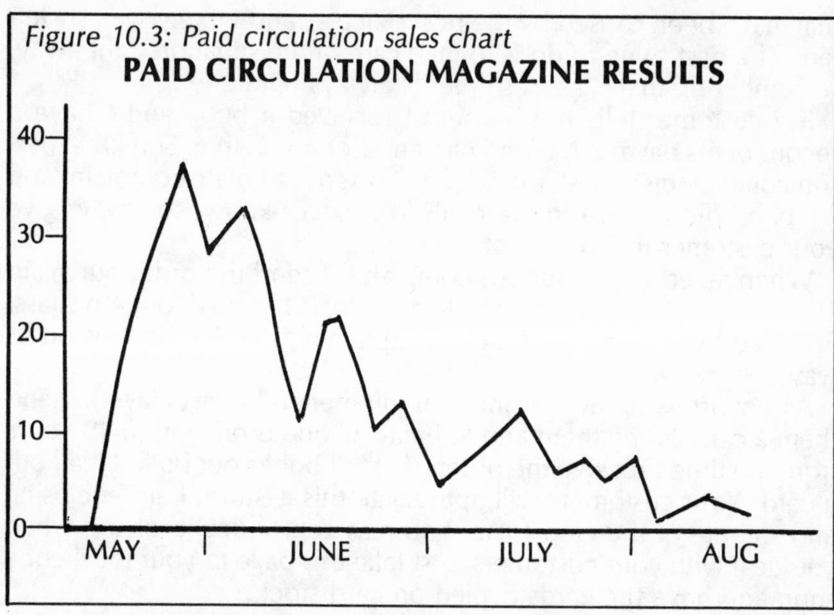

Figure 10.4: Non-paid circulation sales chart

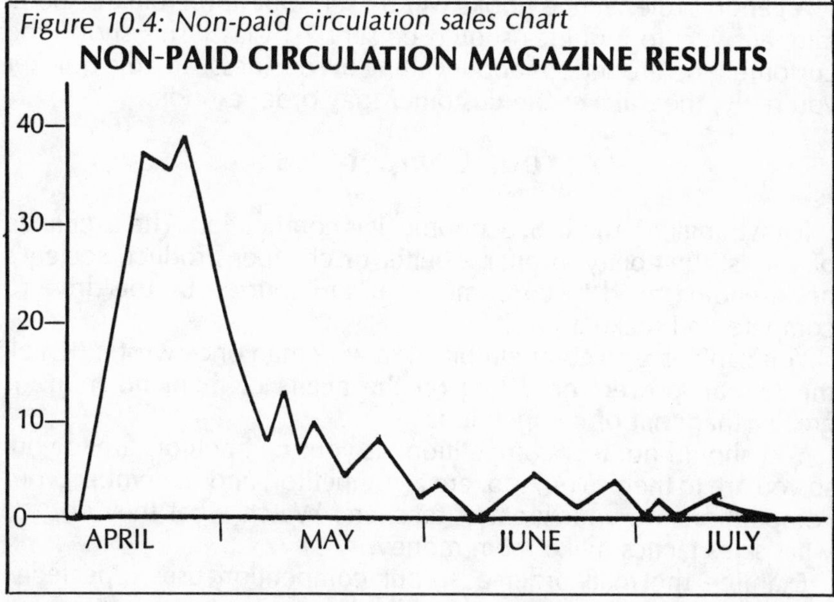

Figure 10.3 and 10.4 show the results by month of advertising a book with a sale price of $6 in two monthly magazines, the first a paid-circulation publication, the second non-paid. Your results should be similar.

may have been caused by the post office — and write you nasty letters. The best thing to do is to take care of the situation right away, remembering that "the customer is always right."

If a customer tells me he hasn't received a book and I have a record of his payment, I send him another book, free. Sure, that person could be dishonest, but what if it was a legitimate complaint and his book did get lost in the mail? You never know, so always give your customer the benefit of the doubt.

When faced with a serious complaint, I send the order out again 1st Class. For less serious complaints, I send the book out 4th Class, followed by a card sent 1st Class explaining that the book is on its way.

As a courtesy to my customers, if shipment is being delayed, I send them a card letting them know. I mail all books out within 48 hours from the time I receive the order. If I mail books out bulk, I mail out a card. Your customers will appreciate this gesture. I am enclosing an example of the card I use. You may reproduce it for use when you deal with your customers. Just take this page to your local copy shop and have the cards copied on card stock.

A general rule: While books will be sent out at the bulk or book rate, answers to inquiries should be sent 1st Class. This shows the customer you are serious about getting his business, and the quicker you reply, the quicker the customer may order a book.

Your Competitors

If anything fires the U.S. economy, it is competition. The exchange of goods, the ability to offer a better or cheaper product, society's never-ending need to consume — all are spurred by the drive to compete and make a profit.

You can't escape competition. As a wise man once wrote: "Of all the human powers operating on the affairs of mankind, none is greater than that of competition."

You should not fear competition; as your competitors are to you, so you are to them. You, too, are a competitor; and remember, your competitiors are your greatest teachers. Watch what they do, see what sales tactics make them money.

Examine the mail order ads your competition uses repeatedly, month after month — only ads which have a good and continuous response are repeated. Learn from these ads.

A success story often cited is Joe Karbo. When he came out with his famous ad for *The Lazy Man's Way To Riches,* his innovations quickly became the norm: requesting post-dated checks that allow

THANK YOU! We have received your inquiry/order

____

____

____

☐ Your order was sent to you ____________________

☐ We were out of stock, but will send ______________

____

☐ No check or money order was enclosed. Please send

____

☐ Please send an additional ____________________

☐ Please send an additional ______________ because of the foreign exchange rate and oversea postage.

☐ Please send a photocopy of both sides of your check or money order or the exact date you mailed your order.

☐ This check/credit card has been declined. Please send ______________ by money order or cash.

☐ Your order will be sent to you immediately after we receive your payment.

Customer Service

Lion Publishing Company
Suite 204, 4776 El Cajon Blvd.
San Diego, CA 92115
Phone (619) 265-8777

Figure 10.5: My inquiry cards

customers time to inspect the merchandise, and using an accountant's sworn statement to back up claims of financial success.

You should also consider ordering your competitors' books, just to see what they're up to and how they make money.

While there will be other mail order book sellers competing for the same market, that market is always growing. Not only is the

The Lazy Man's Way to Riches

'Most People Are Too Busy Earning a Living to Make Any Money'

"... I didn't have a job and I was worse than broke. I owed more than $50,000 and my only assets were my wife and 8 children. We were renting an old house in a decaying neighborhood, driving a 5-year old car that was falling apart, and had maybe a couple of hundred dollars in the bank.

Within one month, after using the principles of the Lazy Man's Way to Riches, things started to change — to put it mildly.

- *We worked out a plan we could afford to pay off our debts — and stopped our creditors from hounding us.*
- *We were driving a brand-new Thunderbird that a car dealer had given to us!*
- *Our bank account had multiplied tenfold!*
- *All within the first 30 days!*

And today...

- *I live in a home that's worth over $250,000.*
- *I own my "office". It's about a mile and a half from my home and is right on the beach.*
- *I own a lakefront "cabin" in Washington. (That's where we spend the whole summer — loafing, fishing, swimming and sailing.)*
- *I own two oceanfront condominiums. One is on a sunny beach in Mexico and one is snuggled right on the best beach of the best island in Hawaii.*
- *I have two boats and a Cadillac. All paid for.*
- *I have a net worth of over a Million Dollars. But I still don't have a job..."*

I used to work hard. The 18-hour days. The 7-day weeks.

But I didn't start making big money until I did less—a *lot* less.

For example, this ad took about 2 hours to write. With a little luck, it should earn me 50, maybe a hundred thousand dollars.

What's more, I'm going to ask you to send me 10 dollars for something that'll cost me no more than 50 cents. And I'll try to make it so irresistible that you'd be a darned fool not to do it.

After all, why should you care if I make $9.50 profit if I can show you how to make a *lot* more?

What if I'm so sure that you *will* make money my Lazy Man's Way that I'll make you a most unusual guarantee?

And here it is: I won't even cash your check or money order for 31 days *after* I've sent you my material.

That'll give you plenty of time to get it, look it over, try it out.

If you don't agree that it's worth *at least a hundred times* what you invested, send it back. Your *uncashed* check or money order will be put in the return mail.

The only reason I won't send it to you and bill you or send it C.O.D. is because both these methods involve more time and money.

And I'm already going to give you the biggest bargain of your life.

Because I'm going to tell you what it took me 11 years to perfect: How to make money the Lazy Man's Way.

O.K.—now I have to brag a little. I don't mind it. And it's necessary—to prove that sending me the 10 dollars... which I'll keep "in escrow" until you're satisfied... is the smartest thing you ever did.

I live in a home that's worth $250,000. I know it is, because I turned down an offer for that much. My mortgage is less than half that, and the only reason I haven't paid it off is because my Tax Accountant says I'd be an idiot.

My "office," about a mile and a half from my home, is right on the beach. My view is so breathtaking that most people comment that they don't see how I get any work done. But I do enough. About 6 hours a day, 8 or 9 months a year.

The rest of the time we spend at our mountain "cabin." I paid $30,000 for it—cash.

I have 2 boats and a Cadillac. All paid for.

We have stocks, bonds, investments, cash in the bank. But the most important thing I have is priceless: time with my family.

And I'll show you just how I did it—the Lazy Man's Way—a secret that I've shared with just a few friends 'til now.

It doesn't require "education." I'm a high school graduate.

It doesn't require "capital." When I started out, I was so deep in debt that a lawyer friend advised bankruptcy as the only way out. He was wrong. We paid off our debts and, outside of the mortgage, don't owe a cent to any man.

It doesn't require "luck." I've had more than my share, but I'm not promising you that you'll make as much money as I have. And you may do better; I personally know one man who used these principles, worked hard, and made 11 million dollars in 8 years. But money isn't everything.

It doesn't require "talent." Just enough brains to know what to look for. And I'll tell you that.

It doesn't require "youth." One woman I worked with is over 70. She's travelled the world over, making all the money she needs, doing only what I taught her.

It doesn't require "experience." A widow in Chicago has been averaging $25,000 a year for the past 5 years, using my methods.

What *does* it require? Belief. Enough to take a chance. Enough to absorb what I'll send you. Enough to put the principles into *action*. If you do just that—nothing more, nothing less—the results *will* be hard to believe. Remember—I guarantee it.

You don't have to give up your job. But you may soon be making so much money that you'll be able to. Once again—I guarantee it.

The wisest man I ever knew told me something I never forgot: "Most people are too busy earning a living to make any money."

Don't take as long as I did to find out he was right.

Here are some comments from other people. I'm sure that, like you, they didn't believe me either. Guess they figured that, since I wasn't going to deposit their check for 31 days, they had nothing to lose.

They were right. *And here's what they gained:*

$260,000 in eleven months

"Two years ago, I mailed you ten dollars in sheer desperation for a better life... One year ago, just out of the blue sky, a man called and offered me a partnership... I grossed over $260,000 cash business in eleven months. You are a God sent miracle to me."

B. F., Pascagoula, Miss.

Made $16,901.92 first time out

"The third day I applied myself totally to what you had shown me. I made $16,901.92. That's great results for my first time out."

J. J. M., Watertown, N.Y.

'I'm a half-millionaire'

"Thanks to your method, I'm a half-millionaire... would you believe last year at this time I was a slave working for peanuts?"

G. C., Toronto, Canada

$7,000 in five days

"Last Monday I used what I learned on page 83 to make $7,000. It took me all week to do it, but that's not bad for five day's work."

M. D., Topeka, Kansas

Can't believe success

"I can't believe how successful I have become... Three months ago, I was a telephone order taker for a fastener company in Chicago, Illinois. I was driving a beat-up 1959 Rambler and had about $600 in my savings account. Today, I am the outside salesman for the same fastener company. I'm driving a company car... I am sitting in my own office and have about $3,000 in my savings account."

G. M., Des Plaines, Ill.

I know you're skeptical. After all, what I'm saying is probably contrary to what you've heard from your friends, your family, your teachers and maybe everyone else you know. I can only ask you one question.

How many of them are millionaires?

So it's up to you:

A month from today, you can be nothing more than 30 days older — or you can be on your way to getting rich. You decide.

Sworn Statement:
"On the basis of my professional relationship as his accountant, I certify that Mr. Karbo's net worth is more than one million dollars."
Stuart A. Cogan

Bank Reference:
Home Bank
17010 Magnolia Avenue
Fountain Valley, California 92708

Joe Karbo
17105 South Pacific, Dept. MM
Sunset Beach, California 90742

Joe, you may be full of beans, but what have I got to lose? Send me the Lazy Man's Way to Riches. *But don't deposit my check or money order for 31 days after it's in the mail.*

If I return your material — for *any* reason — within that time, return my *uncashed* check or money order to me. On that basis, here's my ten dollars.

Name ____________________

Address ____________________

City ____________________

State __________ Zip __________

© 1978 Joe Karbo

Figure 10.6: Joe Karbo's famous full-page ad

percentage of literate people rising, so are personal incomes, use of credit cards and the cost of selling by means other than mail order. There seems no end in sight — the mail order business grosses more than $100 million a year and grows annually between 13% and 18%.

A brief word on the time-honored practice of underselling your competition. There are no rules, except one: Don't do it to drive a competitor out of business — it is sometimes illegal and always unethical.

11

Advertising That Sells

The best ads ever written were well planned before they were created. Planning ahead is very simple and enables you to create impressive ads.

The best advertising agencies use this method, and I'm showing it to you because I want you to create great ads. You may feel you already know all this information, and going through this process may seem unnecessary. But if it works for the best in the business, don't you think it's worth your time?

The following steps will put you in the same "mind set" as the big thinkers in the big ad agencies.

There are several questions you must ask and answer, in writing:
What am I selling?
Who is my target market?
What does my target market want?
How can I reach my target market efficiently?
Does my target market need and want what I am selling?

What am I selling?

You must ask yourself what you are selling. In your case, you are selling a book. Your potential customers will view what you are selling not merely as a book, but as a vehicle, a means to an end. You are offering them information they need for whatever purpose they choose to put it. You are helping them fulfill their dreams and desires.

There are two ways to describe the product or service you are selling: by features or by benefits.

If I describe a pen I am selling by features, I say it is made of plastic, it has a two-year warranty and the barrel is replaceable.

Benefits, however, are what the features mean to the customer. A pen of plastic means that the pen will be durable, will save money, won't tarnish or corrode and is inexpensive. If the pen has a two-year warranty, the customer will save money and have a reliable writing instrument.

As another example, if I sell cameras, what am I really selling? Not just a well-made machine with several ground-glass lens. I am selling memories.

But what about books? If you are selling a book on how to make money, are you merely selling a 200-page book? No, you are selling a system for making money. Similarly, if you are selling a gardening book, you are not just offering a book with color photographs of garden plots and rows of vegetables, but a method of making carrots grow long and tomatoes grow fat — in effect, a system of creating better vegetables.

You have already chosen your book by now, haven't you? I want you to sit down and think. Think about what you are really selling in terms of customer benefits. Write down your findings on a piece of paper.

Who is my target market?

Find out who your potential customers are. Are they male or female? What are their jobs, their goals and desires? To whom does your book appeal?

If your book is about gardening, your market is gardeners, of both sexes, probably single-plot owners who live in semi-urban areas. If your subject is computers, your market is less narrow, probably of medium income and encompassing a wide range of interests. If your subject is how to make money, your market is much larger — enormous, in fact, because everyone wants to know that. If you know your book, you know your market.

Just as in the previous exercise, write down who your target is. Think about it and write this down on a piece of paper below the previous answer.

What does my target market want?

Conversely, if you know your market, you know what book to write or sell. When you know who your prospects are, it isn't hard to know what they want. It's the reverse process of knowing who your target market is.

I will give you an example of determining what your target market wants. First, let's say my target market is low-income people, aged 35 to 55, living in rural areas. Second, I know one of the things that low-income people want: money. What can I sell low-income people? A book on how to get low-interest government loans.

I used this same technique to target my market for the book, *How To Use Your Hidden Potential To Get Rich*. I targeted this book to low-income people and, as a result, I sell about 1,000 copies a month. This adds up to more than $100,000 a year in sales from this book alone.

Write down what your target market wants, just below your observations for the previous exercise.

How can I reach my target market efficiently?

It is not enough to know who your prospects are — you must reach them. And if you can't reach them profitably, you can't undertake your advertising campaign.

You can reach customers through the media. A medium is any vehicle that is used to reach prospects, such as the mail, magazines, radio, television, newspapers, etc.

Magazines that cater to the same specialized audience that your book is aimed at are your best bet. Only advertise in newspapers that specialize in a certain market, i.e. your local newpaper caters to everyone who can read, so avoid it. Instead, *The National Enquirer,* for example, has a largely low-income audience; *The Senior Citizen* specializes in senior citizens. Use specialty papers which are aimed at your market.

Mail order advertisements run in certain states will result in more sales per capita than those run in other states. The key question is, how many people per thousand in a particular state order by mail? The state with the highest mail order response is Alaska. Why? Because many parts of Alaska are isolated, so it is more convenient for many Alaskans to order by mail.

There is a simple way to find out in which publications you should advertise. Look at your competitiors — in which magazines do they advertise? If they keep advertising in the same publication, they must be making money. If they are making money by advertising in a specific magazine or tabloid, so can you.

Also, read the editorial content of magazines — is it aimed at your market? If the magazine is full of stories about coin collecting, your book on pre-War German coins will probably sell well.

Does my market need and want what I sell?

You now know what you are selling, you know what your target market wants. You must now determine if the two match. Your target market must want to buy and read what you are selling.

When you have finished this step you must decide how to sell your book. There are many alternatives — I will discuss each alternative in the next few chapters, but I'll tell you what they are now:

1. Sell your books directly from display ads in magazines and newspapers.

2. Sell your books directly from classified ads in magazines and newspapers.

3. Use a classified ad to entice your potential customer to write you for more information. You then send him your sales literature.

4. Obtain a list of potential customers and send them your sales literature.

5. Use the free publicity offered by magazines, newspapers and broadcast stations.

6. Use a combination of any of the above plans.

I show you in the next few chapters how to use each of these plans to sell your books.

12

Creating The Successful Display Ad

Some of you will decide to sell your book through display ads, one of the most expensive but effective methods open to you. There is big money in running display ads. Karbo and Haroldson made millions using them — they ran full-page ads that pulled in 10,000 orders. Imagine that. Let me go into more detail.

Before you take the display ad option you need to know how much it will cost. Display ads are not cheap: A full-page ad in *Opportunity* magazine costs $3,605, and that's for a one-time run. I have enclosed a sample rate card so you can familiarize yourself with them.

The 15% discount

One thing I want to mention is the 15% advertising discount. Notice the section of the rate card on "commissions, discounts and credit." See what it says on Number 1: "Agency commissions to recognized advertising agencies only — 15%."

D. CLOSING DATES

1. Cover and center spread forms close 15th of second month preceding issue month. (Example: July issue covers and center spread close on May 15th.)
2. Body of magazine except center spread — final forms close 26th of second preceding month. (Example: July issue closes May 26th.)
3. No proofs furnished for correction or changes after 25th of second preceding month. (Example: July issue proof changes not accepted after May 25th.)
4. Cover, center spread and insert cancellations not accepted after 1st of second preceding month. (Example: No cover, center spread or insert cancellations accepted for July issue after May 1st.)
5. No body of magazine cancellation of advertising or changes in submitted copy accepted after 16th of second preceding month. (Example: No inside of magazine cancellations or changes accepted for July issue after 16th of May.)

E. ADVERTISING CONDITIONS

1. Artwork required by advertisement as indicated in layout, billed at cost plus 15%.
2. Orders demanding positions other than covers and center spreads not accepted.
3. We assume no responsibility for film, art or cuts uncalled for six months after date of insertion.
4. Companies unknown to publisher must send full particulars of proposition and credit information.
5. No order accepted until approved by Opportunity Press, Inc.
6. Opportunity Press, Inc. reserves right to refuse any advertising for any reason and to omit accepted advertising which interferes with production schedule due to tardiness of receipt or special demands of advertiser.
7. We assume no responsibility for errors in ad keys.
8. Cost of changes in approved copy after advertisement is in proof form will be billed to the advertiser.
9. No blind advertisement will be accepted until full information on specific purpose and proposition is submitted to Opportunity Press, Inc.
10. Advertisements with box numbered addresses or no street addresses not accepted, unless Opportunity Press, Inc. is supplied with full address and phone number. This information maintained in confidence on request.
11. Advertisers and advertising agencies assume liability for all contents of advertisements printed, and for any claims on OPPORTUNITY PRESS, INC. arising therefrom.
12. Advertisers and advertising agencies agree that OPPORTUNITY PRESS, INC. shall be under no liability whatsoever by reason of any error or omission for which OPPORTUNITY MAGAZINE may be responsible in any advertisement beyond the cost of space actually occupied by the error.
13. Mailing Instructions: Send all orders, copy, layouts and other materials to OPPORTUNITY PRESS, INC., Suite 1405, 6 North Michigan Avenue, Chicago, Illinois 60602.

F. CHARACTER OF CIRCULATION

1. Direct to consumer salesmen, saleswomen, house-to-house agents, both full time and part time, including party plan operators, crew managers, route men, wagon jobbers. Also potential franchisees, independent salesmen, business opportunity seekers, distributors selling to stores and retail outlets for resale. Salesmen servicing big users such as industries, institutions, schools, hospitals, hotels.
2. Locality of Circulation: National, throughout the United States and possessions and Canada.
3. Subscriptions and highly qualified controlled mailing.
4. In circulation last week of month preceding date of issue.
5. Established 1923.
6. Single copy price, $1.50, subscription price per year $12.00 Canada $13.00. Foreign $16.00.
7. Average monthly circulation 190,000, including paid subscription and controlled.

RATE CARD

Effective with April 1984 Issue

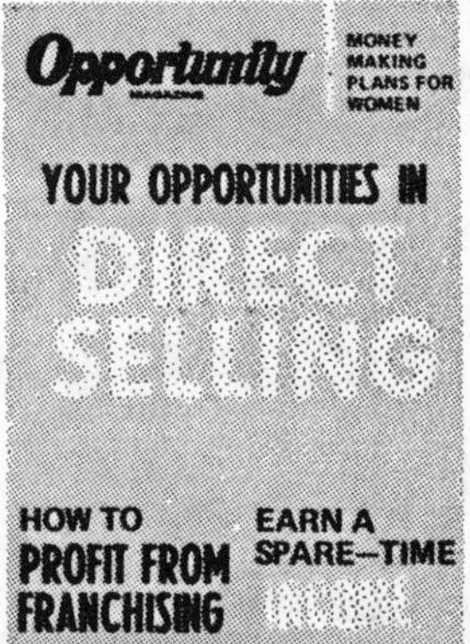

Opportunity
MONEY MAKING PLANS FOR WOMEN
YOUR OPPORTUNITIES IN
DIRECT SELLING
HOW TO PROFIT FROM FRANCHISING
EARN A SPARE—TIME

MONTHLY MAGAZINE FOR SALESPEOPLE, FRANCHISE AND BUSINESS OPPORTUNITY SEEKERS.

A. ADVERTISING RATES
B. COMMISSIONS, DISCOUNTS & CREDIT
C. MECHANICAL REQUIREMENTS
D. CLOSING DATES
E. ADVERTISING CONDITIONS
F. CHARACTER OF CIRCULATION

published by:

OPPORTUNITY PRESS, INC.

GENERAL ADVERTISING OFFICE
Suite 1405, 6 North Michigan Avenue
Chicago, Illinois 60602
312-346-4790
Cable / Salesopp Chicago
Telex / 25-6138

Figure 12.1: Rate card

A. ADVERTISING RATES

DISPLAY RATES SPACE IN AGATE LINES (14 Agate lines equal 1 inch deep by a column 2⅜ inches wide	Wide × Deep	FREQUENCY DISCOUNT (Within 12 Month Period) 1 Issue	6 Issue	12 Issue
14-69	per line	$ 12.50	$ 11.88	$ 11.25
70	(1/6 pg.) ½ Column 2⅜" × 5"	815.00	774.25	733.50
71-142	per line	11.70	11.12	10.53
143	(⅓ pg.) 1 Full Column 2⅜" × 10¼" or 71 lines on 2 columns 5" × 5⅛"	1,650.00	1,567.50	1,485.00
144-213	per line	11.50	10.92	10.35
214	(½ pg.) Standard 5" × 7⅝" 107 lines on 2 columns	2,085.00	1,980.00	1,876.50
214	(½ pg.) Special Vertical• 3⅝" × 10¼" full depth of page	2,160.00	2,055.00	1,951.50
214	(½ pg.) Horizontal 7½" × 5" 71 lines on 3 columns	2,160.00	2,055.00	1,951.50
215-285	per line	10.40	9.88	9.36
286	(⅔" pg.) 5" × 10¼" 143 lines on 2 columns	2,500.00	2,375.00	2,250.00
287-428	per line	8.70	8.27	7.83
429	(1 pg.) black on white 7½" × 10¼"	3,295.00	3,130.25	2,965.50
429	(1 pg.) Black and Red	3,535.00	3,370.25	3,205.50
429	(1 pg.) Black and Special Color	3,605.00	3,440.25	3,275.50
Over 429	per line	7.70	7.32	6.93
858	(2 pgs.) Facing Black on White	6,170.00	5,861.50	5,553.00
PREFERRED POSITIONS*				
429	2nd or 3rd Cover in Black (Color Extra)	3,520.00	3,344.00	3,168.00
429	4th Cover in Black (Color Extra)	3,620.00	3,439.00	3,258.00
858	Center Spread in Black (Color Extra)	6,240.00	5,928.00	5,616.00

COLOR & SPECIAL DIMENSION EXTRAS

(No frequency discount)

Standard Red per page or less $240.00
Special Color per page or less* $310.00
4 Colors* $750.00
Ad layouts across 3 columns
of less than full page space* .... $ 75.00
*When available

SPECIAL 3-TIME CONSECUTIVE INSERTION DISCOUNT

First 2 consecutive insertions at "1 issue" rate. 3rd consecutive insertion only at 10% discount. (If display advertising appears in 6 or more issues within a one year period, the advertiser will qualify for the higher discount, less the amount deducted.)

CLASSIFIED ADVERTISING RATES

Per Word .... $ 3.30
Line of Bold Face or White Space $33.00
Minimum of 12 words $39.60

10% off for three or more consecutive insertions.

Name and address, number groups and initials count as words. Standard setting, first line upper case, balance upper and lower case.

Opportunity MAGAZINE — SERVING THE MULTI-BILLION DOLLAR DIRECT SELLING INDUSTRY

B. COMMISSIONS, DISCOUNTS & CREDIT

1. Agency commission to recognized advertising agencies only — 15%.
2. Payment with order on all accounts whose credit has not been established with the publication.
3. Billing date is on or before the 5th of month preceding month of issue. (Example: July issue advertising will be billed by 5th of June.)
4. Cash discount, 2% on display advertising only, if paid by 15th of month prior to month of issue. (Example: July issue advertising discountable if paid by June 15th.)
5. Account past due on 1st of month of issue. (Example: July issue advertising past due on 1st of July.)
6. Frequency rates apply only to advertisements by advertiser (or wholly-owned subsidiary) within a 12 consecutive month period and in different issues.
7. Billing involving frequency discount will be payable at the "1 issue" rate until the number of insertions required for discount have been placed. Upon placement of required number of insertions, discount applicable to all previous advertising due to frequency of insertion will be credited or refunded.
   Example: Place 6 or more advertisements in 12 months and earn retroactive 6 time rates on sixth insertion. Six time frequency discount totals 5% credit on space charges, exclusive of color costs. Consecutive insertions in 12 issues will qualify for retroactive 12 time rates upon completion of schedule. Twelve time advertisers will earn 10% discount from single insertion rate on space charges, exclusive of color costs.
8. Minimum display space accepted and required to maintain frequency rate — 14 lines (1 inch).

C. MECHANICAL REQUIREMENTS

1. Widths: Single column .... 2⅜"
   Double column .... 5"
   Type page .... 7½" × 10¼" deep
   Trim size .... 8⅛" × 10⅞" deep
2. Type page — 429 agate lines consisting of 3 columns of 143 agate lines deep each.
3. Printing process: Web offset.
4. Binding method: Saddle stitched.
5. Bleed: 8¼" × 11⅛", minimum of 5/16" between live matter and trim.
6. Preferred material: Right reading negatives emulsion side down, positives, reproduction proofs.
7. Acceptable material: Negatives, positives, reproduction proofs, scotchprints. For halftone reproduction in scotchprints or reproduction proofs, forward Black and White glossy photos. Screened halftone copy accepted at advertiser's own risk.
8. Recommended screens and densities:
   a. B/W and/or 2c screen: recom. 85.
   b. B/W and/or 2c density: max. 160%; 2nd color not to exceed 100%. Only one color may be solid.
   c. 4c screen: recom. 120; max. 133.
   d. 4c density; max. 260%.
9. AAAA/MPA/ABP offset standards apply.
10. Rotation of colors: Y, R, B, Blk.
    (Contact Chicago office for 4-color mechanical requirements and offset standards).

Figure 12.2: Rate card

Well, what if you are not a recognized agency, can you still get a 15% commission? The answer is "yes." The commission is given to advertising agencies for creating your ad. As long as you are creating the camera-ready art work, you are entitled to the commission.

If you create the ad you are called an "in-house" advertising agency. Some publications will try to bluff you out of the agency commission. Insist on it, and if you don't get it, don't advertise with that publication. Every now and then I run into a magazine that tries to reject my 15% commission request. I just tell the ad manager that I refuse to advertise with him until I get it. At that point, I get the 15% commission. Always insist on your commission.

One word of caution before I discuss ad writing. It is true that you can save 15% by creating the ads yourself instead of going to an advertising agency. But if you are not a good ad writer you will lose more than the 15% you saved. Make sure you can write good ads before you buy space in a magazine. If you don't feel confident, see what an advertising agency can do for you. If you do decide to pay someone to create your ads, make sure that person has had experience with mail order ads. Also, study the section on advertising in this book so that you can assist the ad writer with some ad writing expertise of your own.

Enclosed is a copy of an insertion order (Figure 12.2) that you would have to send to a magazine if you wanted to advertise with it.

The Display Ad

The structure of your ad is how you put your ad together. What you say and where you say it will make or break your advertising. Here it is:

Attention grabber

This is the headline at the top of your ad; it grabs the attention of the reader and draws him into your message. I describe in detail later how to write effective headlines.

Interest developer

With this, you interest the reader in what you have to say. For example, open with a story, as Joe Karbo did in his successful ad for *The Lazy Man's Way to Riches*:

"I used to work hard. The 18-hour days. The 7-day weeks. But I

Lion Publishing Co.
4776 El Cajon Blvd., Suite 204
San Diego, CA 92115
(619) 265-8777

Order No.

☐ IF CHECKED HERE, THIS IS AN INSERTION ORDER

☐ IF CHECKED HERE, THIS IS A SPACE CONTRACT

DATE

TO PUBLISHER OF

REPRESENTATIVE

PLEASE PUBLISH ADVERTISING OF
FOR

SPACE | TIMES | DATES OF INSERTION

CLOSING:

POSITION			
COPY	CUTS	KEY	
ADDITIONAL INSTRUCTIONS Please do not back up coupon with another coupon		SIZE	
RATE		CIRCULATION	ON SALE
LESS AGENCY COMMISSION ON GROSS	LESS CASH DISCOUNT ON NET	LEFT HAND COUPON	RIGHT HAND COUPON

SPECIAL INSTRUCTIONS:

PLEASE ACKNOWLEDGE

After publication, please send one complete copy of this issue and two tear sheets of this ad to us.

Order issued by:

Figure 12.3: Insertion order

didn't start making big money until I did less — a lot less."

Or, you can start with an unusual or startling statement. For example, Mark Haroldson's ad for *How To Wake Up The Financial Genius Inside You* opens with: "Millionaires are not 100 or even 10 times smarter than you are, but it is a fact that millionaires are making 10 to 50 and even 100 times more than you."

Another example is Charles Abbott's ad selling tips on low-cost legal advice, which opens with: "My name is Charles Abbott. I'm a lawyer myself — and I may be cutting my own throat — but I'm going to tell you the truth."

Benefits of your book

Write down all the benefits your book offers your prospects. (Developing benefits is explained in the section titled "What am I selling?") When you have finished your list, rank each benefit according to importance. The most important benefit will be the theme of your ad; the secondary benefits will be secondary themes in your ad. Think of and include as many benefits as possible.

First, emphasize the main benefit your book offers. Is it making money? Then say so. For example, in his ad, Karbo writes that he has a $250,000 home, boats, stocks and bonds, etc., and he leaves no doubt that the reader can get these things, too.

Trust builder

No matter what you claim, if the reader does not believe your ad, you will not sell.

One way to establish credibility is to use testimonials. For example, for an ad for another book I wrote, *How To Use Your Hidden Potential To Get Rich,* I had my financal advisor attest to my financial success. Under the words "Sworn Statement," he wrote: "I testify that David Bendah has indeed been able to secure an income of $8,254.41 in the first five days of using his systems. (signed) Virgil Holsinger, Financial Consultant, San Diego, California."

Or, to again cite Karbo, who first used the testimonial technique: "On the basis of my professional relationship as his accountant, I certify that Mr. Karbo's net worth is more than one million dollars. (signed) Stuart A. Cogan."

You can also state your bank account and give references, such as your bank or Chamber of Commerce.

In addition, you can use excerpts of letters written to you by

. . . I'm a lawyer myself — and I may be cutting my own throat — but I'm going to tell you the truth:"

Using a Lawyer May Be Dangerous to your Wealth

My name is Charles Abbott. I'm a lawyer myself — and I may be cutting my own throat — but I'm going to tell you the truth:

The bulk of what most lawyers do could be done by someone who had never seen the inside of a law school—and usually is.

Lawyer's *secretaries* do most of the work on wills, divorces (as well as annulments and legal separations), bankruptcies and creditor plans, simple contracts, real estate deals (buying, selling, and leasing), run-of-the-mill personal injury cases, adoptions, filing homesteads, insurance claims, minor criminal cases . . . and the list goes on and on.

And what do these Legal Secretaries do? They follow directions and fill in the blanks on forms. That's all. It's as simple as that.

That's why I think you may be ready to try being your *own* lawyer — and save a 'ton' of money.

But before you decide, answer these two questions: (1) Can you follow simple directions — no more complicated than assembling a Christmas toy or reading a cook book? (2) Do you have the few cents necessary to buy the correct forms at a Legal Stationery Store?

If your answer to both of those questions is "yes," you're *ready*. Well, *almost* ready. There are just two more things you should know:

(1) You don't necessarily have to have "the few cents necessary to buy the correct form at a Legal Stationery Store." Because I'll tell you how and where to get many of these forms *free*.

(2) You'll need my book. It's called "Do Your Own Legal Work." (And you *can* do your own legal work — no matter which State you live in!)

The book took more than a year to write. Based on what I've actually been earning in my law practice, that represents more than $100,000 worth of advice.

I mention that, not to brag, but so you'll know that I'm not some kid, fresh out of law school, and hungry for a few bucks. Along that line, you should know that I have a juris doctor degree in law, that I've been practicing for 13 years, and that I've written the book about the legal problems I work with, day in and day out.

Some other things you might want to know: I've published technical legal articles that explain the law — to lawyers. I've served as a research assistant to a Judge of the U.S. Circuit Court of Appeals. In addition, my biography appears in the prestigious Marquis' "Who's Who in American Law."

What will it cost you to "hire" a lawyer with those qualifications? Ten dollars. Just about what I—and lots of other lawyers—would charge you for 10 *minutes* of legal advice.

Why so cheap? Because I hope to sell a million copies—or at least enough so I can take some time off and enjoy life with my family.

That's what's in it for me.

And here's just a sample of what's in it for *you* (including complete directions and sample forms you can practice with):

How to find and use forms . . . page 7

How to draft your own will . . . page 36

How to handle your own criminal case . . . page 72

How to settle your own accident or personal injury case . . . page 82

How to handle an adoption . . . page 99

How to dissolve your marriage . . . page 113

How to solve debt problems —from consumer-credit counseling to bankruptcy . . . page 127

How to draft a contract . . . page 289

How to handle real estate transactions . . . page 216

How you can use a Law Library—free—to avoid probate! . . . save taxes! . . . form a corporation! . . . and handle hundreds of other matters! . . . page 25

Now I'm not saying that you're never going to need a lawyer. I *am* saying that if you do need to see one, you'll be *ready* and be able to handle a lot of the simple, clerical work yourself. You'll save *his* time.

Here's an example of how my book will cut down on those precious minutes: For an attorney to draw up a simple contract might cost you $400 if he had to start from scratch. It could cost you $30 if he had to take only a half hour to review the work you'd already done —and *can* do, using my book.

Lawyers get $60 for husband-wife wills; I'll show you how to do your own in less than an hour. Lawyers charge $450 for a simple divorce which may take less than two hours of their time. Lawyers get between $3,000 and $4,500 for obtaining a $9,000 personal injury settlement. I'll show you how to do as well, or better, by yourself. Lawyers get $150 for an adoption, but their secretaries do the work — and so can you.

You still may be a little skeptical, so let me share just a few comments from other people:

Followed easy instructions and saved $300.00

"Everything you say is true. I started by going to a lawyer, but he charged me $56.00 for a half-hour visit and one phone call — with no results! Then I got your book. I followed your easy instructions and took care of my problems myself, *AND* saved $300.00 in additional attorney's fees. Needless to say, I am very satisfied, and feel everyone should have your book."

B.P., Benton Harbor, Michigan

"Sincere thanks"

"I have been looking for such a publication for many years to help me educate myself on various legal issues and requirements. Please accept my sincere thanks for bringing out such a fine guide for the non-legal mind."

V.S., Penang, West Malaysia

"Valuable information and answers"

"Today I got from the mail your book which contains valuable information and answers which enlightened me with my problem. I want you to know too that I'm greatly impressed with your guts and admire your honest objective."

E.G., Los Angeles, California

"It is well worth its price"

"I have purchased your book entitled "Do Your Own Legal Work," and found it quite interesting and enlightening. It is well worth its price."

M.C., Wampum, Pennsylvania

"Save our members thousands of dollars in legal fees"

"I have found your book to be most helpful. I have completed my trust and wills . . with savings of over $200.00 in attorney's fees.

We have a movement pending through our credit union to save our members Thousands of Dollars in legal fees through the use of your book."

C.D.M., Nine Miles Falls, Washington

Your best guarantee that my book is everything I say it is, is this: My fellow lawyers will be watching me like a hawk. I wouldn't dare mis-step or mislead you. It could cost me my license.

What's more, I'm so sure you'll find my book *immediately* profitable — that I'll let you read it without paying for it!

Here's how you can read my book without any risk at all. Go ahead and order, my book by mail. Keep it 30 days and read and check it out. Feel free to show it to a lawyer or anyone else you want. Then if you are not 100% satisfied, send it back and my publishing company will return your entire payment to you quietly and without question.

If you want to play it extra safe, you can post date your check or money order by 30 days. If you do that I personally guarantee that my publishing company will not deposit your money for *at least* that amount of time. Then, if you decide to return the book, the company will send back your uncashed check or money order with no questions asked.

There's no way you can lose. Your book will be sent promptly by return mail. If you have any questions, you can telephone (801) 224-6508. Checks and money orders should be made payable to Advocate Publishers. It is not a good idea to mail cash.

© F. P. Publishers, Inc., 1977

Advocate Publishers, Dept. MM
256 South Robertson
Beverly Hills, California 90211

Prove it to me. Show me how I can hire a $100,000-a-year lawyer for 10 dollars. I've enclosed my check or money order—but don't deposit it until the date shown on the check. If I return your book within 30 days, send my payment back. I understand my order will be processed the day it's received.

I enclose $10.

Name____________________

Address____________________

City__________ State__________ ZIP__________

Figure 12.4: Charles Abbott's full-page ad

satisfied customers, making sure you don't use their full names and addresses without their written permission.

Action

Your ad should end with a call to immediate action. In his ad, Karbo even goes so far as to call his readers fools if they do not respond immediately: "What's more, I'm going to ask you to send me 10 dollars for something that'll cost me no more than 50 cents. And I'll try to make it so irresistible that you'd be a darned fool not to do it ... A month from today you can be nothing more than 30 days older — or you can be on your way to getting rich. You decide."

Apart from urging them on, you can compel readers to respond by offering a limited-quantity offer (this offer is never false), a limited-time offer ("Good for two weeks only") or a special ("Free gift sent with all orders"). In addition, you can say that the price of the book will rise soon, due to increased costs, etc.

The Headline

The most important part of your ad is the headline; in fact, research shows, 80% of an ad's success depends on it. Your headline is your main attention grabber.

So what in a headline makes it a success, makes readers stop at your ad instead of flipping on through the magazine? It must arouse the reader's curiosity, appeal to his self-interest and stress the most important benefit of the book. Add to these characteristics words such as "free," "rich," "introducing," "new" and "easy" and your headline becomes a powerful psychological tool.

You must understand the concept that "people want to know what you can do for them." If there is nothing in your headline for them, they will not respond to it. The headline should tell your prospects what you are going to do for them; it must portray a definite benefit.

Here is an example of a poor headline, one that lacks reader benefit:

It's Fun To Make Money The Easy Way

A person will read this, agree with it, perhaps think "no kidding," and move on to the next page. Compare it to this headline:

You Can Make Money the Easy Way

Apart from the headlines of Karbo and Haroldson that I've already shown you, here are some successful heads:

How To Win Friends and Influence People
How To Flatten Your Tush
Everything You Always Wanted to Know About Sex But Were Afraid To Ask
The Power of Positive Thinking
The Amazing Diet Secret of a Desperate Housewife
How To Make Love To A Single Woman

Another type of effective headline is one that not only appeals to self-interest but also asks a question. The reader's curiosity moves him to read the ad. Here are some examples:

How Would You Like To Make Big Money?
Do You Want Higher Wages?

Now that you know what factors make a good headline, how can you know what to put in yours? What should your headline stress? It's simple. The most powerful benefit your book has to offer should be in your headline. That is why I wanted you to write your body copy before you wrote your headline. Pick out the major benefit mentioned in your body copy for a dynamic headline.

Words That Sell

Here are more words and phrases that, when included in your headline, will give it punch: free, guarantee, save, discount, money, make money, easy, profit, prosper, compare, announcing, special, now, you, introducing, modern, low cost, startling, advice, how to, why, value, wholesale, solution, sale, sensational, amazing.

If you are still not sure how to write headlines like the ones shown, study the headlines of ads that are repeated month after month in mail order magazines or newspapers. You should also start a file of good and bad ads to give you a constant reference of "do's" and "don'ts."

The Subhead

The subhead is located just below or just above the headline, in smaller type. It is written using the same techniques as headline writing; its main purpose is to expand on the headline and further draw the reader into your ad. Examples are:

Gold Jewelry
Your Quick Way To Easy Money

Big Profit Sales
Get Moneymaking Benefits
Work Part or Full Time
Free Booklet

In addition to the main subhead near the headline, subheads are often scattered over the page. They break up large blocks of copy, and are therefore a useful design tool; they highlight the secondary benefits your book offers.

Look at Melinger's ad in figure 12.4 — notice all the subheads and headlines he uses.

Capturing Your Target Audience

If you know your target audience, and by now you should, you can write your headline and subheads to appeal to that narrow market. The headline appeals to the prospects' self-interest and states a benefit; the subhead gives more detail and states a second benefit. For example, if your book is about pet care:

PET OWNERS CUT COSTS
New Book Shows How to Save Money, Keep Pets Healthy

The headline catches the attention of all pet owners and states the primary benefit: saving money. The subhead gives more detail and states the secondary benefit: keeping pets healthy.

Ad-Writing Tips

Of course, the advice I gave you on the structure of your ad doesn't cover the whole topic. Here are some more tips:

The "you attitude"

All your ad copy should contain the "you attitude." This tells your readers that you are interested in them, rather than only in yourself.

FREE SAMPLE MAILED TO YOU TO PROVE EVERYTHING I SAY IS CRYSTAL TRUE

MEN WOMEN get rich in the MAIL ORDER World Trade Business

B. L. MELLINGER, Famous World Trader, Internationally known Mail Order Expert.

"I started in Mail Order a few years ago, part time in my garage. I had less than $100. I discovered how to make Mail Order pay big. Today my business empire spans the globe. My Plan lets you use my experience to make a fast start in your own big profit home business."

START AT HOME — Immediately! — Same Day You Receive My Profit Plan

You can start fast. I reveal Mail Order product winners, how to Buy Below Wholesale for biggest profits, how to make little ads that bring orders. With my confidential Drop Ship Plan you need no capital. Sell party plan or to stores. Deal direct with overseas suppliers. You keep all profit.

Make your first Mail Order transaction 10 minutes after you open my Plan. Keep your regular job or income. Spare time home Mail Order profits can go to savings, travel, luxuries. Great for husband/wife teams, family projects or retirement plans. Mail Free Sample Coupon below.

BUY BELOW WHOLESALE

24,221 IMPORTS

You get early news for over 24,000 new imports a year that you can sell by mail. My foreign travels uncover newest imports. I show you how easy it is to deal direct with the supplier, cut out middlemen, keep all the profit!

3 WAYS TO MAKE MONEY! PICK ONE OR ALL. I SHOW YOU HOW

MAIL ORDER
Mailman Brings Orders Filled With Cash
SECRETS now revealed... Turn your spare time into big profit Home Mail Order Business. Start without big capital investment.

IMPORT
BUY BELOW WHOLESALE
Fantastic foreign values create instant sales. I search out new imports. Put you in direct contact with suppliers. Drop ship plan starts you with little or no capital.

EXPORT
Cash-In-Advance Orders
Start home Export business. Export products made locally. Get cash in advance orders from foreign buyers. I reveal new export leads. Local firms hungry for export orders.

READ WHAT OTHERS SAY . . . MONEY MAKING REPORTS

9 Valuable Aids for BIG PROFITS

Four Generations in World Trade

START WITH 24,221 PRODUCTS!

Many you can buy one at a time or order in quantity. Example: one 35 mm camera with hot shoe and carry case $13.00 ppd or 12 for $7.41 ppd. Price drops to only $5.80 in larger quantities. New government ruling makes thousands of imports free of any duty whatsoever. You deal direct my International Traders way. Cut out greedy U.S. specialty merchandise middlemen. Really deal direct.

FREE MEMBERSHIP
Free International Traders Membership. World wide organization gives you a full staff of I.T. consultants to help you build in U.S. and overseas.

FOREIGN SUPPLIER CONTACTS
My 25 years foreign travels set up a network of overseas friendships. You benefit from inside contacts. I open doors so you can Buy Below Wholesale, often in small quantities!

FREE Catalogs

DOUBLE PROFITS
As a Member of International Traders, you will also get free catalogs of specialty merchandise to order at rock bottom prices from our big U.S. warehouse.

Personal Computer $232
Includes Keyboard, Ram Pack, Printer, Recorder, Monitor, Joystick, Software.

The Mellinger Co., 6100 Variel Avenue, Dept. T2363
Woodland Hills, CA 91367-3779

FREE SAMPLE COUPON

The Mellinger Co.
6100 Variel, Dept. MM
Woodland Hills, CA 91367-3779

Send Free Sample Import & Free Report . . . Show me how I can start a Mail Order World Trade Business of my own. I understand there is no obligation and no salesman will call.

IMPORTANT
I agree to limit my request to only one Free Sample Import. I have not previously requested this Free Sample. I am 18 years or older.
Initial here______

Name ______________ Age ______
Address ______________
City ______________
State ______________ Zip ______

Save 3 days, give ZIP for fast reply

MARCH, 1985 · 5

Figure 12.5: B.L. Melinger's full-page ad

Here are some examples of sentences with and without the "you attitude":
Without: Earn up to $50
With: You can earn up to $50
Without: I can make dreams come true
With: I can make your dreams come true

Positive atmosphere

Never say anything negative in your ad. Never tell people what they can't do, only what they can do. If you only have a red and blue product, not yellow and green, don't tell your prospects that you don't have yellow and green — tell them you have red and blue.

Here are two examples of negative statements made positive: "You shouldn't be poor" should read, "You should be rich"; "Don't drive around an old clunker" should read, "Drive a new Mercedes."

Present tense

Studies show that ads using the present tense have the greatest selling impact. Use the present tense in all your ads, not the past or future tenses.

Captions under illustrations

If there are any illustrations or pictures in your ads, put captions under them. A reader's eyes are automatically drawn to illustrations, so capitons that go with those illustrations get high readership.

Simplify your writing

Avoid long sentences. Your ad should be as easy as possible to understand, so limit sentences to 20 words. Write as if your audience is a class of seventh-graders

Words to use

Every word in your ad should be understood by everyone who reads it, so use simple and familiar words that convey your message quickly. Here are some examples of difficult words commonly found in ads and their easily understood alternatives:

utilize	use
ascertain	find out
substantial	a great deal
majority	most

The same rule applies to phrases — make them simple and omit needles words. For example:

he is a man who	he
the reason why is that	because
owing to the fact that	because
in spite of the fact that	although

Again, if you have problems writing simply and with vigor, a good reference is Strunk and White's *The Elements of Style,* available at bookstores for about $4.

Test your ad for clarity

If you are unsure whether your writing can be easily understood, test it out on an average 12 year old. Ask him if he can understand what you wrote; if he can't, ask which words, phrases or paragraphs confused him. Write down what he tells you and rewrite your ad.

Offer free information

It is difficult to get people to send more than $20 from a full-page ad unless they know who you are or have bought from you before. The amount of money you ask for is proportional to the amount of space you allow for your sales talk. If you are asking more than $20 for your book, even a well-written, full-page ad in a large-circulation magazine may not bring great success. Instead, buy a small add and offer free information about a given topic; with that free information, send sales literature about your book.

Ads offering free "how-to" information succeed because they arouse curiosity; they prompt a response because the reader has nothing to loose.

Be sure to put the offer of free information first, the sales talk second.

Specialty Merchandise Company uses this technique in its ad, which entices you to send away for a free booklet. When you receive the free booklet, the company tries to sell you its complete wholesale kit, which costs close to $200.

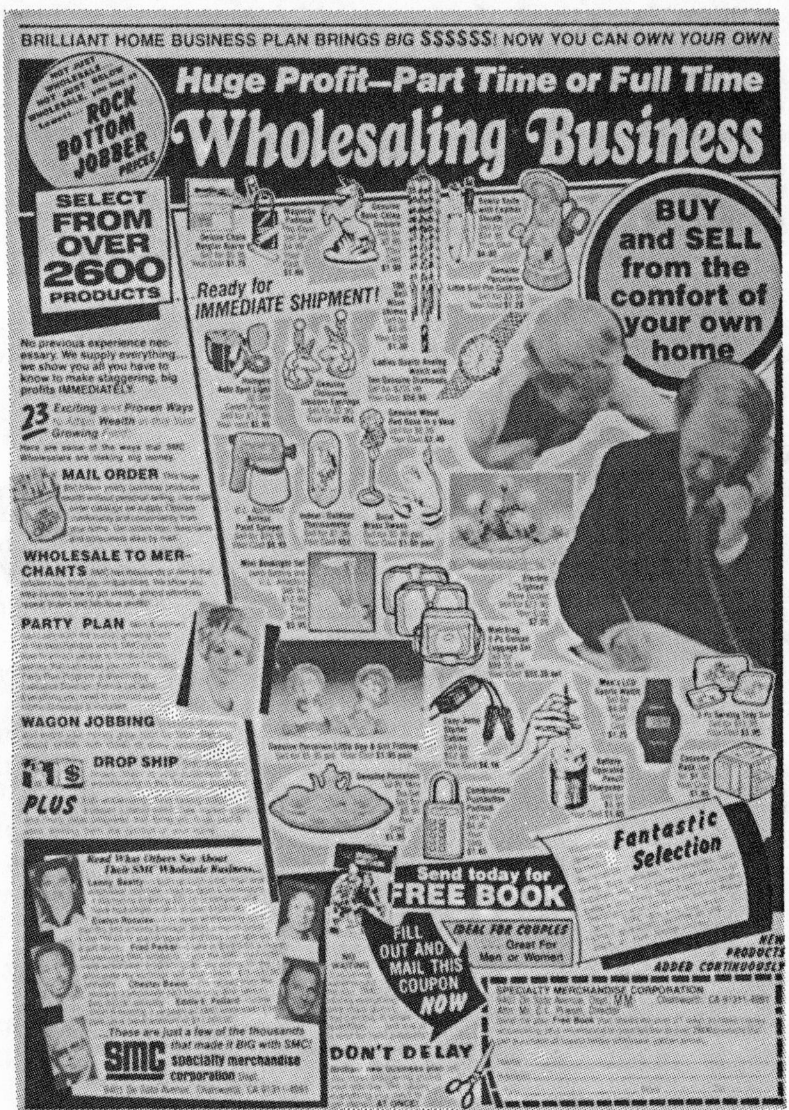

Figure 12.6: Specialty Merchandise Company's full-page ad

Use long copy

As a general rule, the more copy you have, the more prospects you will get. But you won't be able to sell if you merely repeat the same ideas over and over — you must introduce new and different benefits.

Make your copy dynamic

I have mentioned this before, but I want to remind you again to use short words, short sentences and short paragraphs.

When you reread and edit your ad, pare it down, cut unnecessary or repeated words, and write conversationally, as if talking excitedly to a friend.

Advertise your book only

If my ad prompts more people to buy soft drinks, I have increased the primary demand for soft drink. If my ad gets more people to buy COKE, I have increased the secondary demand for soft drink. You are not trying to increase the primary demand for books, you are not trying to get people to buy more books in general. What you are trying to do is increase the secondary demand for books, to get people to buy just your book.

The point I am trying to make is that when you are advertising a book on dieting, don't talk about the merits of losing weight — talk about how your particular book can help your potential customer. If you just talk about losing weight in your ad, your potential customers will go out and join a health spa and forget about buying your book. You must convince them that your book is the best solution to their weight problem.

Because you don't have a monopoly on the self-publishing mail order book market, make sure your ads zero in on your book only; your ad shouldn't promote all books that are of the same general topic as yours.

Professional touches

To give your ad that final professional touch, put your logo at the bottom. You may also consider including an order form for your book on the bottom right corner of your ad. Order forms make it easier for your customer to order your book.

Stimulate quick responses

Apart from a free-information, limited-quantity, limited-time or special offer, there is another popular method of getting readers to order your book as soon as they finish reading your ad.

Offer a free, inexpensive, but attractive gift for all orders received within a certain time, say 10 days. It will increase sales because the lure of anything free prompts procrastinating prospects.

Anything that makes ordering more convenient will result in a quicker response, so include a coupon with your sales literature or ad. *Reader's Digest,* for example, includes a pencil with each subscription renewal. This way, prospects don't have to search for a pencil, so there is little danger of putting off the task until later and ultimately putting it off forever.

Money-back guarantee

A "satisfaction guaranteed" assurance and a "money-back guarantee" are now a standard and necessary practice. You will experience few serious complaints or returns unless your book is of poor quality.

Post-dated checks

With post-dated checks, you wait 30 days before taking the check to your bank. Your customer is then assured of satisfaction before payment. It also means you must send the book before the check clears.

The major problem with this guarantee is that you will likely receive many bad checks, as many as 10% of your total. Some dishonest people have 500 checks printed, then close their account. They then send checks to every company they can think of. With banks charging you $2.50 for every bad check you deposit, that's a large loss to absorb. But, by offering the post-dated-check guarantee, you should increase sales by enough to cover your losses from bad checks.

Here is what I have done to reduce my bad checks by up to 75%. I joined TeleCheck's new mail order division. Just placing the TeleCheck logo in my ad scares off bad check writers. All you do is log each check you receive, pay TeleCheck about 4% of the amount of the check and the firm covers it, even if it bounces. As a free service, TeleCheck places your bad checks in its negative data bank; then, when a person who wrote you a rubber check tries to write

FREE GRANTS

LOW INTEREST LOANS

• NO COLLATERAL • NO CREDIT INVESTIGATIONS • NO CO-SIGNERS

Did you ever wonder how people with a credit rating less than yours obtain money? The only difference between them and you is that they know how and where to get the money. Every year billions of dollars are given to people just like you. Would you like to stake your share? You can get your share by owning one of the most complete books on money financing systems. It shows you how to get money from almost every possible source available. Hundreds of methods of raising money are covered in this book.

$5,000 to $500,000

Learn How To

- Get up to $500,000 from easy to qualify SBA loan
- Get up to $350,000 if you're handicapped in bus.
- Get up to $315,000 for low income assistance
- How to get completely out of debt, without bankruptcy
- How to raise $50,000 with no collateral
- Borrow up to $100,000 from any commercial bank
- Raise up to $50,000,000 the corp. way.
- Buy apts and homes next to nothing
- Get up to $67,000 for house purchase
- Get up to $5,000 a year for education
- Get up to $92,000 for house improvements
- Get up to $150,000 if you're a woman in bus.
- Raise $200,000 with your signature as collateral
- Loopholes to get you around the policies of banks
- Use creative financing systems to raise large amounts of money
- Use advanced banking techniques to get loans
- 270 Foundations that will give you a grant
- Get some of the 3 billion given out by foundations every year
- 300 Financial institutions that loan by mail

These are just some of the money raising techniques included

©1985

FREE BONUS

I will include a free report on how you can enter a $100,000 a year business with no investment. You can become a money broker. This report is my free gift to you

MY GUARANTEE TO YOU..

Postdate your check for 30 days. That will give you enough time to apply for your grant or loan. Your check that I will hold for 30 days will be returned to you if you don't get the money you need. Why am I so confident that I can offer you this guarantee?

For the past five years, I have helped over 15,000 people get the money they need.

Yes, I want to know almost every source and method I can use to obtain free grants and low-interest loans. Send me your fully documented book on the condition that you don't deposit my payment for 30 days. If I can't get the money I need, return my payment to me.

On that basis, here is my $6.00

TeleCheck®

NAME ______________________

ADDRESS ______________________

CITY__________ST______ZIP______

Federated Financial Services
Suite 300, 5515 Jackson,
La Mesa, CA 92041 Dept. MM

Figure 12.7: Federated Financial Services ad

another to one of TeleCheck's 85,000 dealers in Canada and the United States, the check is rejected. If you don't want to join TeleCheck, just have the company process your checks through its negative data bank — it's a free service.

HOW TO WIN FRIENDS AND INFLUENCE PEOPLE

JOHN D. ROCKEFELLER, SR. once said: *"The ability to deal with people is as purchasable a commodity as sugar or coffee. And I will pay more for that ability than for any other under the sun."*

Wouldn't you suppose every college would conduct practical courses to develop this "highest-priced ability under the sun"? To our knowledge, none has.

How to develop that ability is the subject of Dale Carnegie's book.

A few years ago Chicago University and the United Y.M.C.A. Schools made a survey to find out the prime interest of adults. The survey took two years, cost $25,000. It indicated that their first interest is health—and their second, how to understand and get along with people, how to make people like you, how to win others to your way of thinking.

Wouldn't you suppose that after the members of this survey committee had decided to give such a course, they could readily have found a practical textbook? They searched diligently—yet could find none suitable.

The book they were looking for was published not long ago. Almost overnight it became a best seller. It is one of the fastest-selling books published in the twentieth century. More than 805,000 copies have been sold to date! It is outselling any other non-fiction book in America!

The Man Behind the Book

This book is called *How to Win Friends and Influence People* - and is written by the one man who is perhaps better qualified to write it than anyone else.

Dale Carnegie is the man to whom the big men of business come for practical guidance on the subject of getting along with people, dealing with them successfully, winning others to their own way of thinking. During the last 26 years he has trained more than 22,000 business and professional men and women—among them some of the most famous in the country.

When he conducts his course in Public Speaking and How to Influence People in the ballroom of the Hotel Commodore, or The Pennsylvania, or the Hotel Astor (the second largest hall in New York) the place is packed to capacity. Large organizations—such as The New York Telephone Co., Westinghouse Electric and Manufacturing Company, and many others listed elsewhere on this page—have had this training conducted by Mr. Carnegie in their own offices for their members and executives.

This book, *How to Win Friends and Influence People*, grew and developed out of that vast laboratory of experience. As you can judge from the panel at the top of this advertisement, it is as practical as 26 years of actual successful experience with the problems of thousands of people in all walks of life can make it.

Consider the Case of Michael O'Neil

Michael O'Neil lives in New York City. He first got a job as an automobile mechanic, then as a chauffeur.

When he got married he needed more money. So he tried to sell automobile trucks. But he was a terrible flop. He suffered from an inferiority complex that was eating his heart out.

On his way to call any prospect he broke out into a cold sweat. Then, before he could get up enough courage to open the door, he often had to walk up and down in front of an office half a dozen times.

When he finally got in he would invariably find himself antagonizing, arguing. Then he would get kicked out—never knowing quite why.

He was such a failure he decided to go back to work in a machine shop. Then one day he received a letter inviting him to attend the opening session of a Dale Carnegie course.

"It may do you some good, Mike, God knows you need it"

He didn't want to go—he was afraid that he would be out of place—that there would be a lot of college men there. But his despairing wife made him, saying, "It may do you some good, Mike, God knows you need it."

He went to the meeting, and other meetings of the course. He lost his fear. He learned how to talk effectively and convincingly, how to make people like him at once, how to win friends and influence others.

Today Michael O'Neil is a star salesman for one of the country's largest manufacturers of motor trucks. His income has mounted and skyrocketed. Last year at the Hotel Astor he stood in front of 3,800 people and told a rollicking story of his achievements. Few professional speakers could have equalled his confidence—or his reception.

Michael O'Neil is a salesman—but his problem was exactly the same as that of thousands in other fields—the fundamental one of getting along with people. The way it was solved is just one example of what Dale Carnegie's help has meant to more than 22,000 others of his students in all types of endeavor. *What Dale Carnegie has done for them he can do for you.* Look at the chapter headings. They indicate the amount of hard-hitting, priceless information Dale Carnegie's book contains. But the subject is so intensely important that we say, look at this book without obligation. Then decide whether or not you want to own it.

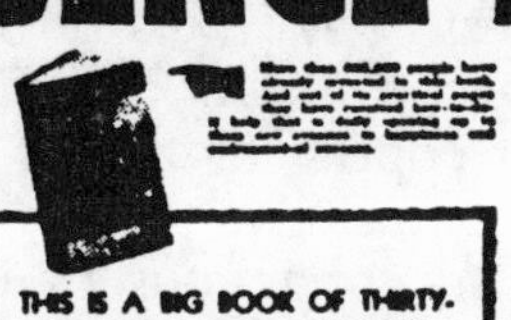

THIS IS A BIG BOOK OF THIRTY-SEVEN CHAPTERS, INCLUDING:

- The Big Secret of Dealing with People
- Six Ways to Make People Like You Instantly
- An Easy Way to Become a Good Conversationalist
- A Simple Way to Make a Good First Impression
- How to Interest People
- Twelve Ways to Win People to Your Way of Thinking
- A Sure Way of Making Enemies—and How to Avoid It
- The Safety Valve in Handling Complaints
- Do This and You'll Be Welcome Anywhere
- How to Get Cooperation
- A Formula That Will Work Wonders for You
- The Movies Do It. Radio Does It. Why Don't You Do It?
- Nine Ways to Change People Without Giving Offense or Arousing Resentment
- How to Criticize—and Not Be Hated for It
- How to Spur Men on to Success
- Making People Glad to Do What You Want
- Letters That Produced Miraculous Results
- If You Don't Do This, You Are Headed for Trouble
- Seven Rules for Making Your Home Life Happier

DALE CARNEGIE

Dale Carnegie is the man the men of business come to for practical instruction in getting along with people. During the last 26 years he has trained more than 22,000 business and professional men—more than any other living man.

Large organizations such as

Westinghouse Electric & Manufacturing Co.	Brooklyn Chamber of Commerce
New York Telephone Co.	Philadelphia Chamber of Commerce
Bell Telephone Co. of Pennsylvania	Philadelphia Electric Co.
American Institute of Electrical Engineers, New York	Philadelphia Gas Works Co.
McGraw-Hill Publishing Company, New York	Carrier Engineering Corporation
	Philadelphia Association of Life Underwriters

have had this training conducted in their own offices for their members and executives.

This book is a direct result of Dale Carnegie's experience, the only working manual of its kind ever written to help people solve their daily problems in human relationships.

SEND NO MONEY

Try Dealing THIS WAY with People —just for FIVE Days!

This book is sweeping the country. It is on every best-seller list. It is one of the largest-selling books of non-fiction of the twentieth century!

When you get your copy simply read it; there are no "exercises" to be practiced. Then try for five days Dale Carnegie's simple method of dealing with people. Judge for yourself, in your daily social or business life, how easily whatever you do, say, or write can win the friendship and the hearty cooperation of others—instead of arousing resentment, friction, and either a negative response or no action at all.

It is not necessary to send any money now. You may pay for *"How to Win Friends and Influence People"* when it is delivered—with the definite understanding that the price of only $1.96 will be refunded to you if you wish it. If this book does what we claim, it will mean more to you than *ANY* book you have ever read. If it doesn't, we do not want you to keep it. Mail the coupon at the left at once.

SIMON and SCHUSTER, *Publishers*
386 Fourth Ave. New York City

ONLY $1.96 *If you decide to keep it!*

SIMON and SCHUSTER, *Publishers*
Dept. 109, 386 Fourth Ave., New York City

Please send me How to Win Friends and Influence People. I will pay postman only $1.96 plus few cents postage charges. It is understood that I may read it for 5 days and return it for refund if I then feel that it does not in every way live up to the claims made for it.

Name

Address

City State

☐ Check here if you prefer to enclose $1.96 WITH this coupon. In that case WE will pay the postage charges. The same refund privilege applies of course.

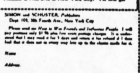

Figure 12.8: Victor Schwab's famous full-page ad

Increase Your Advertising Knowledge

How To Write A Good Advertisement

The more books on advertising you study, the better you will be at writing ads. One book I especially recommend is *How To Write A Good Advertisement, A Short Course In Copywriting,* by Victor O. Schawb, one of the best copywriters of this century. He created many famous ads — one, for *How To Win Friends And Influence People,* sold 5 million copies for author Dale Carnegie. I have reprinted this ad for you to study.

Schwab's techniques are continuously studied by the top advertising agencies, and you should study them, too. Instead of focusing on the stucture of the successful ad, Schwab concentrates on the psychology of the consumer. If you know what consumers want and need, your ads will do very well. After reading his book, you should be able to pin-point the precise needs of your customers and know how to fulfill them. You can pick up this 227-page, 8½-by 11-inch book at most fine bookstores for $16. If you have trouble finding it, I can ship it to you within 48 hours for only $16, including postage and insurance. Just write to Lion Publishing.

13

Dollars In Your Mailbox With Classifieds

Many people starting out in mail order choose classified advertising to sell their books. I highly recommend taking this route because it is the safest and often the cheapest.

Many years ago a women placed a classified ad in a publication for a $1 recipe book called *101 Ways to Fix Hamburger*. She received $10,000 for her effort. This is just one small example of the success other people have enjoyed from classified ads.

Classifieds are the easiest to create — you don't have to be a brilliant copywriter or do any layout or artwork. All you have to do is follow my instructions for creating winning classified ads.

The main reason people use classified advertising is to save money — other than word-of-mouth and free publicity, classifieds are the cheapest ads money can buy. But they can also be the most rewarding. You don't risk thousands of dollars every time you advertise and they offer the best dollar-for-dollar return. A dollar spent on classified advertising brings in far more money than a dollar spent on any other form of advertising.

As with all advertising methods, classifieds have their particular disadvantages: They have the least visual impact; they provide little space for details about your book; they leave no room for a sales pitch and offer.

Also, your ad must compete with hundreds of others on the same page that look almost the same as yours. You will not be able to use artwork and will probably not be given a choice of typefaces, other than bold face or size of type and headline. In other words, there is little you can do to attract a reader's attention — you have only a split second to catch his eye as he skims the page, so how and when you use this selling tool is very important.

How Much You Should Charge

You will not be able to get more than $4 for a book through a classified ad, but the price depends on how useful or unique you book is. To be on the safe side, don't use classified ads to sell your book directly to the customer if you want more than $2 for it.

In other words, don't say "Send $10 today for your book" because no one will. In the limited space available in a classified ad, you have no room for a sales pitch and people will not chance sending $10 for something they know little about.

Instead, if you're asking more than $2 for your book, use the "two-step" method.

The Two-Step Method

The two-step method involves prompting your potential customer to write you for sales information about your book. For example:

BIG PROFITS. New book reveals secret of wealth. Work home. Guaranteed. Free details: Lion Publishing, 4776 El Cajon, 204B, San Diego, CA 92115.

To entice your potential customer to write you, offer in your classified ad either free information or a free (inexpensive) gift. Not surprisingly, the free-gift ploy draws the most response.

With this two-step method, which is used by all the mail order experts, the reader is likely to respond because he has nothing to loose. Then, when you send him the requested information, include sales literature on any other books you also sell.

A successful variation of this two-step method is to ask your potential customer to send you 10 to 25 cents or a postage stamp to help cover the cost of sending out information. This will cut down on your responses, but means those you do get will be from serious customers, those likely to buy your book. Remember that some people send away for anything as long as it's free, and are not really interested in your book. Asking for a small payment should weed them out.

One rule you should follow if you ask for a token payment: Only do so if (a) the sales literature you send out costs you more than 75 cents an order (including postage) and you are asking less than $50 for your book; or, (b) your classified ad reaches a very wide audience.

Where To Run It

Classified ad sections that capture the widest readership in newspapers are "Business Personals," "Personals" and "Miscellaneous." Pick a category that fits your needs.

In addition, the newspaper or magazine may have other categories that suit your purpose and will narrow your audience to only those readers likely to buy your books. These are: "Books, Periodicals," "Moneymaking Opportunities," "Help Wanted," "Employment Information" and "Mail Order Opportunities."

To know if you should run your ad in a certain publication, see if it carries ads similar to yours. If a competitor advertises in that publication on a regular basis, it means he is making money. Advertise in it.

I know of one company that can get you a combined rate for magazine and tabloid classified advertising. Your ad is inserted in many different magazines and you are charged one flate rate. The company does all the work and you pay no extra. Write for a free catalog: National Mail Order Classified, P.O. Box 5M, Sarasota, FL 33578.

When To Run It

Newspapers

Run your classified ad in the Friday, Saturday or Sunday editions of newspapers — those are the most carefully read, especially Sunday. Also, afternoon papers are better than morning editions.

If your book appeals to a wide audience, newspaper classifieds are a cost-effective medium. If it appeals to a narrow, specialized audience, magazines classifieds are a better bet, but newspapers allow you to:

1. Get your ad on the street fast; within a couple of days of ordering it, you can reach a lot of people in a limited area.

2. Advertise your book relatively cheaply, depending on the newspapers's circulation.

3. Change the wording of your ad often, to test which has the best result.

Newspapers, especially daily newspapers, are a bad medium to use for your mail order product. Unless your book has a wide appeal, stay away from daily newspapers.

Magazines

The most effective months for magazine classifieds are the same as for display ads. Refer to the section "When Should I Sell" in Chapter 10.

Choose in which magazines to run classifieds the same way you choose in which magazines to run display ads, covered in Chapter 11 in the section "How can I reach my target market efficiently?" Also, the magazine research you did to find information for your book has a second use: It tells you which magazines attract readers interested in your book's topic. Place your classified ads in the most popular of these, or the most specialized, depending on your book.

For even more magazines, ask the reference librarian for *Standard Rate and Data, Ayer Directory of Publications* and *Ulrich's International Periodicals Directory* — they list every magazine by subject and circulation. Look through these directories for publications that meet your needs.

In addition, for a list of addresses, advertising rates and circulation figures, you can order the *Directory of Magazines with Classified Ads* from SpeciaList, 134 Manchester Road, Baldwin, MO 63011.

All magazines will answer advertising questions; some will send you a free sample copy on request.

When You Will Get Your Orders

You can expect a quarter of the responses from a classified ad run in a monthly magazine to come within a week after you receive the first order. Half your responses will arrive within a month of the first order received.

Expect a different response rate with a weekly magazine or

newspaper: Half the responses will come within two weeks after the first order. Weekly magazines and weekly newspapers will always do better for you than their daily counterparts.

Newspapers and weekly magazines have a very short life. People usually throw them away as soon as they read them. The longer the publication is laying around, the better your response will be.

Writing Your Classifed Ad

Remember the discussion in Chapter 12 on how to write headlines and ads, about how to grab the reader's attention, hold it and spur him to action? All the same rules apply for classifieds.

The use of short words and sentences is even more important in classifieds than in display ads, mainly because publications charge you by the word or by the line. Most magazines charge by the word while daily newspapers tend to charge by the line.

For example, the successful classified ad I run for this book is:

BIG PROFITS. New book reveals secret of wealth. Work home. Guaranteed. Free details: Lion Publishing, 4776 El Cajon, 204B, San Diego, CA 92115.

Notice the "B" after "Suite 204." I use a different letter for each magazine I advertise in; when the order is received, the tag letter tells me which ad the customer responded to. This in turn tells me which ads and which magazines are effective.

Use this simple formula to find the cost to you of each reply to your ad:

Cost of ad/number of replies = cost per reply.

Use this formula to find the cost to you for each actual sale:

Cost of ad/number of sales = cost per sale.

Of course, the cost per sale is the most important, as you will generate different numbers of replies based on how you word your ad.

For example, a "blind" ad generates a lot of inquiries but fewer sales. It promises much, fails to specify what you are selling and peaks the curiosity of many readers who will ask for details but may not buy your book.

BIG PROFITS. Proven methods. No soliciting. Free details: Lion Publishing, 4776 El Cajon, 204B, San Diego, CA 92115.

Classified — MARKET

INCOME OPPORTUNITIES—is published monthly. The rate per word for CLASSIFIED ADVERTISEMENTS is $4.95 payable in advance—minimum ad $74.25. Capitalized words 40¢ per word additional.

ACCOUNTING & TAX SERVICE

OVERPAYING YOUR TAXES? Individuals and businesses; little known LEGAL tax strategies can save YOU thousands. Reply to: American Tax Strategies, Inc., P.O. Box 1065, Dept. I. Findlay, Ohio 45839.

ADDITIONAL INCOME

HOMEWORKERS needed painting novelties. Fun and easy. Earn good profits. Free details. Write: N. Roland, Box 56-IO, Hammonton, NJ 08037.

ASSEMBLE OUR DEVICES (Electronic). We send parts and pay for assembly. Beginners welcome. Write. Electronic Development Lab, Box 1560D, Pinellas Park, Florida 33565.

END Financial worries. Make more money than you ever imagined at home. Information: Stadar House, Inc., 10 Canterbury Circle, Madison, WI 53711.

AGENTS WANTED

EVERYONE A PROSPECTIVE CUSTOMER. Show our line of Fast Selling Belt Buckles, Badges and Accessories to Truckers, Police, Firemen, Postal Carriers, Taxi and Bus Drivers and others. Personalizations available. Over 7,500 Emblems available. Hook-Fast, Box 1068-IN, Providence, RI 02901.

50% off colorful hot-foil printed business cards. Catalogue $9.95. Signet, 50 High St. LL70, Buffalo, NY 14203 VMCAE.

SINCERE BOOK SALES AGENTS WANTED NOW! Part-Time or Full. Do not confuse with usual worn-out offers. No experience needed. Full Details send $1.00 to: DSA Publishers, 11514 Ventura Blvd., Suite #109, Studio City, CA 91604.

AVIATION

ANTIGRAVITY PROPULSION DEVICE! Free Brochure. RDA, Box 873, Concord, NC 28025.

BARGAINS

IMPORTED jewelry and bargain books. Quality products at low cost. Send $1.00: Deb Car Products, P.O. Box 8700J, Dept. 1284, College Park, GA 30337.

BLUEPRINTS, PATTERNS & PLANS

NEW CRAFT PRINT CATALOG—Choose from over 100 great easy-to-build plans. Send $1.50 (completely refunded with your first order). BOAT BUILDER, (CP Div.)—380 Lexington Ave., New York, NY 10017.

BOOKS & PERIODICALS

PUBLISH YOUR BOOK! Join our successful authors. Publicity, advertising, beautiful books. All subjects invited. Send for fact-filled booklet and free manuscript report. Carlton Press, Dept. SML, 11 West 32 Street, New York 10011.

MAKE YOUR CLASSIFIED AD PAY. Get "How to Write A Classified Ad That Pulls" Includes certificate worth $2.00 towards a classified ad in this publication. Send $2.25 (includes postage) to I. M. Bozoki, Davis Publications, Inc., Dept. CL, 380 Lexington Ave., New York, NY 10017.

NEW RELEASE 1985 ENTREPRENEUR'S HANDBOOK FOR SUCCESS. Profitable Ideas, Inside MLM, Sales Plans, Marketing Guide, Success Formulas, and More! $5.00: Exsellors, 111 Robin Road, #241, Somerville, N.J. 08876.

MAKE MONEY taking pictures for post cards. BOOKLET, complete details $2.75: Houston Post Card Company, P.O. Box 266958, Houston, Texas 77207-6958.

BUSINESS OPPORTUNITIES

VENDING MACHINES. No selling. Routes earn amazing profits. 32-Page Catalogue FREE. Parkway Corporation, 1930NO Greenspring Drive, Timonium, Maryland 21093.

BUSINESS OPPORTUNITIES—Cont'd

YOUR OWN RADIO STATION! AM, FM, Cable, licensed, unlicensed, low cost transmitters! Free information! BROADCASTING, Box 130-GO72, Paradise CA 95969.

$700 PER MONTH earnings possible filling out income tax forms at home or tax office during tax season. We show you how. Simple, quickly learned. Details mailed free. No salesmen. Hurry. Big Demand. Federated Tax, 2037 Montrose, Chicago 60618.

HIGH PROFITS WITH CUSTOM T-SHIRTS AND CAPS. Inexpensive, professional heat transfer machines. All supplies. PRESS MAGIC, P.O. Box 22809 (BC), Tampa, FL 33623.

GET RICH!! Secret law smashes debts—brings Cash. Credit! Details FREE! Wealthkit-V12, Billings, NY 12510.

INCREASE YOUR INCOME! Help arrange loans, leases, other financial services through nationwide lender network. Prestigious "money" business, full/part-time. Top commissions, complete training, continuous support. PFA, Box 697-D, Dana Point, CA 92629, (714) 240-0405 Ext. 100-D.

BELTS and Buckles. Complete line fast sellers including Truckers, Motorcycles, Wildlife, Westerns, etc. Big Profits. Complete dealer set up. Color catalog $1.00. Anchor Specialties, Box 3958-B10, North Providence, RI 02911.

PIANO Tuning can be learned in six weeks at home! Big profits. Free information. Empire School, Box 1014, Jupiter, Florida 33458.

BORROW $30,000 without interest! All eligible. Repay anytime. Free details! Infohouse-IO 808 Post, San Francisco, CA 94109.

REAL ESTATE FORECLOSURES: REPRESENTATIVES NEEDED for this profitable business. No cash required. Free information. Horizon Financial Corporation, 2474 North Federal H'w'y, Dept. A1, Pompano Beach, FL 33064.

OWN Your Own Business. A successful singles correspondence club. Magazine, details, Free. Destiny Syndicate, Box 5637-BC, Reno, Nevada 89513.

CLIP newspaper items—$2-$25 Each!! FREE report! Clippings (V12), Billings, NY 12510.

SCREEN PRINT T-SHIRTS. Inexpensive kits. Free Details. "T-Printer," POB 23991(BC), Tampa, FL 33623.

MAILORDER OPPORTUNITY: Sell Moneymaking Reports. Reprint Rights included. Make 1000% profit! DETAILS FREE! Write: Venture IO, Box 336, Riviera, AZ 86442.

SELL SENSATIONAL LOW-COST BURGLAR ALARM. Lightning seller. Exceptional margin. Samples for trial. Northwest Electric-IO12, Box 1046, Mitchell, S. Dak. 57301.

PROFITABLE GOLD FOIL PRINTER. Personalize business cards, pencils, matches. Free Details. Gold, POB 24986(BC), Tampa, FL 33623.

STAY HOME! MAKE MONEY ADDRESSING ENVELOPES. VALUABLE GENUINE OFFER. 20¢. Write Lindco, 3636-DA Peterson Ave., Chicago, IL 60659.

BUMPER STICKER PRINTING DEVICE. Cheap, Simple, Portable. Free details: Bumper, POB 22791 (BC), Tampa, FL 33622.

EARN up to $5,000 monthly as a Real Estate foreclosure rep. No license or experience required. National Company provides complete assistance. For info write: Real Estate America, 1601 Main, Plainfield, IN 46168.

$1,000 Weekly Home Business Directory. Free Details. Name and address to: Box 1610-IO, Darien, Connecticut, 06820-1610.

EARN BIG MONEY! Agents needed nationwide. Easy to sell proven product. Steady, repeat orders. National firm trains, supports. Network, Box 6489-D, Laguna Niguel, CA 92677.

BUSINESS OPPORTUNITIES—Cont'd

SEIZED IN GOVERNMENT NARCOTICS RAIDS!! Automobiles . . . Vans . . . Boats . . . Furniture . . . TVs . . . Stereos . . . Thousands other items. Buy Dirt Cheap — Resell for Big Profits! Free Information: Marcel, Box 7557-F, Monroe, LA 71211.

COUNSELORS NEEDED, millions want credit! Fantastic earnings! No experience! Be 1st!: Equal Opportunity Foundation, Box 10323, Marina Del Rey, CA 90295.

BARGAINS! Buy Wholesale and Below! Name Brands. Appliances . . . Furniture . . . Sports Equipment . . . Televisions . . . Cameras . . . Watches . . . Jewelry . . . Thousands More. Free Details. Write Today. Bargainhunters Opportunities, Box 730-IO. Holland, MI 49423.

HIGH Income Sales Positions for collection agency. Free career guide and details. NCC, 781 W. Oakland Park Blvd., Suite 123, Dept/A1, Ft. Lauderdale, FL 33311.

$360 WEEKLY/up, Mailing Circulars! No Quotas/Limits. Sincerely Interested, Rush stamped envelope to: Marketing International, Box 15967-F12, San Diego, CA 92115.

SAVE ON GROCERIES and earn money multi-level, 1500 products. No selling. Send two stamps: Treasure 103-W Potter, Belleville, Mich 48111.

BIBLES! BIBLES! BIBLES! We've expanded our DeVore and Hertel Bible to include New Testaments, small hand Bibles, Giant Print editions, Bible story books and Bible Tapes. Write for our colorful brochures and low prices direct from the publisher. Dept. H, Fireside Bible Publishers, Box 118, Wichita KS 67201.

BE YOUR OWN BOSS. Operate profitable janitorial business Unlimited opportunities. Free details. National Information Services, P.O. Box 61401, Vancouver, Washington 98666.

SELL Books by mail. 400-900% profit. Free Sales Kit. Speedibooks, 23800-2B, Aurora, Bedford, Ohio 44146.

TAKE CATALOG ORDERS. We dropship 2500 best-selling specialty products. Lowest below wholesale prices. Immediate delivery. Spectacular home business opportunity. FREE BOOK. SMC, 9401 De Soto Ave., Dept. 155-48, Chatsworth CA 91311.

GUARANTEED $1.00 per envelope secured, stuffed. Free Watches. Details: Rush pre-stamped, addressed envelope: Watches, Box A-669, Starke, FL 32091.

EARN EXTRY MONEY full or part time. Free information: M. Bailey Publishers, 823 West 10th Street, Freeport, Texas 77541 DptI-1.

PROFITABLE PUBLISHING, PRINTING mailorder business for sale. $12,500. Owner retiring. Rare Opportunity. Eureka, Box 43-BL, Georgetown, CT 06829.

START PROFITABLE BUSINESS AT HOME. GREAT MONEYMAKING OPPORTUNITY. FREE INFORMATION. Michaud Publishing Company, Dept. 53, P.O. Box 244, Orono, Maine 04473.

ALUMINUM SCRAP—Recycle Yourself — MAKE $25.00/POUND! Free information: Industrial Scrap Yard — IO412, Box 127, Alexandria Bay, New York 13607.

MAKE Money working at home! Be flooded with offers!! Details rush stamped addressed envelope & 25¢ service fee: Andrews Distributing, P.O. Box 67, Dept. M, Big Flats, New York 14814.

DISCOVER how to INCREASE YOUR INCOME, be your own boss, ACCOMPLISH ANYTHING! FREE DETAILS! UGOTAHAVA Publishing, #5 Springwood, Box 147, Dept. Z, Greenville, IL 62246.

MAKE MONEY BY THE MINUTE around the clock for doing 8 hours a week paperwork from home. Grows to lifetime income. Totally new ultra-modern project unlike anything before. Still ground floor. No experience or education requirements. 10,500 people already doing. Division of major U.S. corporation. For details dial (216) 452-2171, 24 hrs., 7 days. Ask for ext. 106.

THERE IS NO CHARGE FOR THE ZIP CODE—PLEASE USE IT IN YOUR CLASSIFIED AD

Figure 13.1: Classified ads

Notice that it has fewer words and therefore costs less than the two following ads. It will prompt many replies from the merely curious, but fewer from people likely to buy your book.

A "partially qualified" ad gives the reader more idea of what your are selling, but not a complete picture.

$4,000 A MONTH! Make big money with proven methods. Book reveals secrets. No soliciting. Free details: Lion Publishing, 4776 El Cajon, 204B, San Diego, CA 92115.

This ad will attract fewer inquires than the blind ad, but the ones received will be of "better quality," meaning they are from people quite likely to buy your book.

A "qualified" ad tells the reader exactly what you are selling.

$4,000 A MONTH! New book reveals proven methods of mail order success, self-publishing. No soliciting. Free details: Lion Publishing, 4776 El Cajon, 204B, San Diego, CA 92115.

With this ad, you will receive replies only from people who are very likely to order you book.

Notice that all the examples say "Free details." If you don't charge for your brochure, or offer a free gift as an incentive, you will get many inquiries — remember that some people will send away for anything if it's free. You must decide whether to charge money for your brochure, and it depends on the subject of your book.

If your book appeals to a specialized audience, offer free details or a (cheap) free gift. If it appeals to a wide audience, ask for a nominal fee — this will ensure you get only serious replies.

Classified Ad Guide

Here is an opportunity you may want to try. Davis Publications, the firm that publishes the magazine *Income Opportunities,* offers a book for classified ad writers called *How To Write A Classified Ad That Pulls.* If you buy the book, you get a $2 voucher good toward a classified ad in *Income Opportunities.* I've read the book and it's good. For your copy, send $2.25 to: I.M. Bozoki, Davis Publications, Inc. Dept. MO, 380 Lexington Ave, New York, NY 10017.

14

Making Direct Mail Work For You

A quarter of all books — an amazing one out of every four — are sold through direct mail advertising. Not only are many books sold this way, but buyers are willing to pay more for books that are advertised and sold by mail. In addition, you don't have to compete with the big publishing houses in bookstores.

The first step in a direct mail campaign is to know your product (your book) and know your market (your potential customers), and to make sure they match. See Chapter 11 for a complete explanation of the process.

The first major advantage of direct mailing is the ability to define exactly and locate your market. It's not always easy reaching the type of people you want. For example, say your book is a business guide for minority executives. How do you reach them through an ad campaign? Can you think of any magazines that cater soley to minority executives? There aren't any that I know of which accurately pin-point this segment of the population.

But you can get a list of the names and addresses of thousands of members of any group of executives (or nearly any other group, for that matter), broken down by job, income, age and marital status;

Your Direct Mail Costs

Use this chart to estimate your direct mail costs.

OPERATION	COST PER 1,000	TOTAL COST
1. Artwork and Creation	______	______
2. Mailing Lists (Rental)	______	______
3. Printing Brochure	______	______
4. Printing Letter	______	______
5. Printing Business Reply Card	______	______
6. Printing Business Reply Envelope	______	______
7. Printing Outer Envelope	______	______
8. Folding Brochure	______	______
9. Folding Letter	______	______
10. Labeling Mailing Piece	______	______
11. Inserting	______	______
12. Tie, Bag, Mail Mailing Pieces	______	______
13. Postage/First/Third Class	______	______
14. Total Cost	$______	$______

	TOTAL COST
15. Cost of Product	______
16. Fulfillment, Shipping, Postage Cost	______

17. Total Fulfillment, Product Cost Per Order—Line 15 Plus Line 16	$______
18. Number of Orders Received	______
19. Total Cost for Orders Received Line 17 Multiply Line 18	______
20. Total Mailing Promotion Costs Line 14	______
21. Overhead—Salaries, Phone, Rent, Etc.	______
22. Total Cost for Refunds	______
23. Total Uncollectables/Selling Price	______
24. Grand Total Mailing Programs Costs Add Lines 19, 20, 21, 22 & 23	______
25. Number of Inquiries	______
26. Per Order of Inquiry Costs Line 24 Divided by Line 18 or 25	$______
27. Cash Received per Order	______
28. Total Cash Received Line 18 Times Line 27	______
29. Total Mailing Program Costs Line 24	______
30. Net Profit for Mailing Program Subtract Line 29 from Line 28	$______

Figure 14.1: Chart for figuring direct mail costs

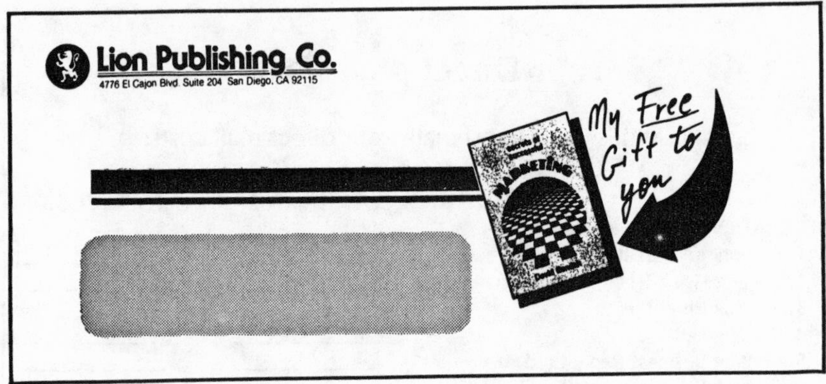

Figure 14.2: Direct mail envelopes

The envelope

The purpose of the envelope is to prompt your potential customer to open it. You can tempt him using several techniques.

a) The teaser. Printed on your envelope is a "teaser," a phrase designed to tempt your potential customer without explaining much. For example, "I made a MILLION BUCKS last year — I'll show YOU how to do the same!" Or, "Would you spend $1 a week to cut your taxes by $1,000?" Or, "You may already have won a fabulous gift!"

b) The blank envelope. Another method is to leave the front of the evelope blank, except for the recipient's name and address. Your potential customer will open your envelope to satisfy his curiosity — if he doesn't, he'll never know who sent it or if it's important.

c) The "confidential" letter. The words "confidential" or "personal" on envelopes are meant to get the letter through the business person's secretary, who usually throws "junk mail" in the trash. Be careful here — this technique definately strains your credibility if there really is nothing confidential or personal in the evelope.

d) The "official" letter. Envelopes that look official, as if sent from the government or a lawyer, are also effective, because the recipient will think it important enough to open. However, more than the "confidential" letter, this method damages your credibility, perhaps irreparably.

The sales letter

The sales letter sells your book, so it is very important to let it do its job. The same rules apply here as with display ad copy: Concentrate on the benefits of your book, write as you talk, use short words, short sentences, be interesting and friendly, but not insincere. If you think you should, refer back to Chapter 12.

Use the format of a letter so that it looks, as much as possible, like a personal letter. Use a date and wide margins. If you have a computer or word processor, start the letter with "Dear Mr. Smith"; if not, try "Dear Coin Collector" or "Dear Fellow Gourmet Cook."

Feel free to emphasize important features of your book with words in **bold** or *italics* or <u>underlined.</u> Make sure the type is large enough to be easily read. Studies have found that letters with a personal touch do better than "generic" messages. You can also highlight important points by writing them out in cursive.

Don't repeat yourself, but don't worry about writing too much. Just write enough to sell your book. It's a common myth that sales letters should be very short and to the point. They should be to the point, but there's nothing wrong with a four-page letter. Some 10-page sales letters have been very successful.

Here's a tip for your sales letter: Always use a P.S. because a P.S. is always read. Make it short and to the point and use it to restate an important benefit of your book.

You may also include a "second chance" or "publisher's" letter. It says something like, "Don't read this unless you've decided not to buy" and then goes on to repeat the sales pitch. The letter should express surprise that the potential customer is not interested in your book; it should restate the facts that it is of high quality and that there is absolutely no risk involved in ordering because of the various guarantees.

The circular

The sales letter does the selling and the circular or flier does the telling. Ideally, it has big, brash headlines and easy-to-read copy printed on glossy paper. It should shout out your message and the advantages of your book. It should, if possible, have an illustration or photograph from or of your book.

It's more visually exciting than the sales letter and serves to reinforce the sales pitch started by the letter. This is usually the most expensive part of a mailing package.

LOS ANGELES BANK
BANK OF AMERICA

MEMBER
FOREIGN TRADE ASSN. OF SO. CALIFORNIA

The Mellinger Co. *Exporters – Importers*

TELEPHONE (213) 884-4400 • CABLE: OVRHAUL •
6100 VARIEL AVENUE • WOODLAND HILLS, CALIFORNIA U.S.A. 91367

I'll show you how to buy below wholesale and deal direct the International Traders way!

From B. L. Mellinger
President, The Mellinger Co.

Dear Friend:

It is with great pleasure that I send you my new full-color book. I know how serious you are about starting your own business. You want the very best help and advice. You want a Plan that makes big money for ambitious men and women. You want to know you have a strong organization backing you!

As you read my book...and I ask you to read it carefully...you learn first-hand how only the world-wide facilities of the Mellinger organization and International Traders can make it possible for you to Buy Below Wholesale ...the one sure way to go after rich profits--quickly, operating directly from your home.

See how you have the benefit of our firm's 60 years of experience...spanning four generations. My grandfather and father both pioneered in Mail Order and World Trade. I personally offer you over a quarter century of great success in World Trade. By following my Plan and my direction, you cash in on years of experience!

- In the pages of my book, you see how I regularly travel all over the world...visiting factories in far-off trade centers, making special arrangements for you with top-quality overseas suppliers, so they will ship you the best new imports at the most favorable prices...even one item at a time.
- AND with my Plan, you DEAL DIRECT WITH THE SUPPLIER by mail. This means you keep all the profits and don't have to share your earnings with some specialty merchandise wholesaler or jobber.

WARNING! Watch out for people claiming to sell you Below Wholesale! If any specialty merchandise jobber tells you he can sell to you Below Wholesale, he is lying and this makes all his other claims doubtful too! This person has bought Below Wholesale from the original supplier, added on a heavy profit for himself and is reselling to you. I make no commission on deals you set up with the fine overseas suppliers I introduce you to. Be smart. Do your business my International Traders way. Deal Direct with the original supplier and keep all the big profits for yourself!

(please turn page over)

Founded 1920, organized in present form by B. L. Mellinger, Jr. in 1947.

Figure 14.3: Sales letter

- 2 -

EIGHT SAMPLE IMPORTS START YOU FAST

I'll send you 8 Free Sample Imports...plus six exclusive Trade Agreements and drop ship offers covering thousands of dazzling imports. I make it easy! Read exactly how you can make your first import transaction only 10 minutes after my Plan arrives.

You don't have to invest a penny in stock or merchandise. My exclusive Drop Ship Plan takes care of that...you can literally "start on a shoestring"!

But let's get one thing straight. I am not asking you to buy anything on what I've said here. All I am asking you to do is mail the Inspection Request on my money-back agreement.

> The day I receive your Inspection Request, I will ship your complete 5-volume Mellinger World Trade Plan--all 20 sections --plus the big 11-piece Visualizer Kit. Inspect the Plan in the quiet of your own home. Show it to friends. Talk it over with your family. If you are not completely satisfied, just mail it back within 7 days of receipt, and I will refund your deposit in full.

This may be the most important day in your life, as far as cash income and future security are concerned. If you want to start making extra money at home - possibly more than you have ever made before, send your Inspection Request at once. I'm waiting to help you get started now!

SEND YOUR INSPECTION REQUEST TODAY--AIRMAIL REACHES ME OVERNIGHT!

Sincerely,

Brainerd L. Mellinger
President

P.S. "Give a man a loaf of bread and you feed him for a day. Teach him how to bake and you feed him for a lifetime." Men-Women, when I show you how to buy over 24,000 products BELOW WHOLESALE, I will give you the opportunity for big earnings for the rest of your life. Send your Inspection Request today, sure!

BACKGROUND OF THE MELLINGER COMPANY:

The Mellinger family has been successfully engaged in World Trade and Mail Order since near the turn of the century. Grandfather Louis Mellinger started in Mail Order in the early 1900's. His son, B.L. Mellinger, Sr., opened his Mail Order business in 1920 and retired to California, a wealthy Mail Order man in 1942. B.L. Mellinger (Jr.) after mustering out of the U.S. Army in 1945, started in Mail Order and from a modest beginning, has built the world-wide organization now known as International Traders. Today, a fourth generation of the Mellinger family, Brainerd L. Mellinger, III, is working with his father, carrying on the tradition in Mail Order which seems destined to span the 20th Century. This family background of success and integrity is the foundation of International Traders. It offers newcomers to World Trade/Mail Order a feeling of security and reliance so valuable to have when entering a new venture of opportunity.

further breakdowns list minority executives by religion (Jewish, Catholic, Muslim, etc.), education (college or high school graduate), interests (conservation, golf, hunting, etc.).

Being able to break down your market to this degree gives your mailing great precision, resulting in the greatest possible number of sales.

The second big advantage of direct mail is the extra space you have for your sales pitch. You are not limited to a single-page display ad, or to a few words in a classified. Your direct mail "package" could include a multi-page letter, a flier, an order blank, testimonials and a guarantee card. All these things, which I detail further on in the chapter, give you more opportunity to push your book.

The third major advantage is the personalized approach. You can tailor your mailer to your target group, including things that appeal particularly to members of that group. If you have a word processor, you can also address each direct mailing piece to the individual person, using his or her name on the envelope — this definately increases response because the potential customer is much more likely to open the envelope. In fact, when I use this technique, I send brochures personalized with the names of those who wrote to inquire about my book. This increases my response 68%.

It's Great For Testing

It is expensive and time consuming to test an ad in a magazine because ads cost a lot and you must wait about six weeks for results. But there is a cheaper and quicker way: direct mailing. There are times when I have to test out five different ads to find which is the most effective. This is how I do it, quickly and cheaply: I create four flyers and mail them to about 400 people each. I then wait for results. I get half the responses within one month, 95% within two months and all within six months. After one month, I can tell which ad is best and so I push forward with that campaign.

What Kind Of Profit You Can Expect

It is important to understand the economics of direct mail. An industry rule of thumb is that a book of wide interest advertised to an average-buying audience will produce a 1.5% to 2% response. In other words, for every 100 pieces you mail, you will receive 1.5 to 2 orders; for every 1,000 pieces, 15 to 20 orders; for every 10,000, 150 to 200, etc.

To do well in direct mail your campaign should bring in orders totaling 2.2 times what the campaign cost you. For example, if your

n Family Sweepstakes News

Latest Edition on Sweepstakes Winners and Potential Winners

AFP AMERICAN FAMILY PUBLISHERS

Founded and Sponsored by: Time, Incorporated and the McCall Publishing Company.

mily Publishers Announces America's First By-Mail
ED MULTI-MILLION DOLLAR SWEEPSTAKES OFFER:

DAVID BENDAH, A LOCAL SAN DIEGO RESIDENT
MAY HAVE ALREADY WON
ONE MILLION DOLLARS!

SAN DIEGO.

David Bendah may soon be receiving guaranteed payments of $50,000.00 every

EXTRA!!! DAVID BENDAH MAY HAVE JUST WON A SECOND MILLION DOLLARS!!!

Figure 14.4: Personalized mailing piece

campaign cost $1,000, you should bring in $2,200 to justify your time and effort. For this, you need a high-priced book, good sales literature and a specialized list.

The cost of reaching each potential customer through direct mail is much higher but much more cost efficient than with display or classified ads. I have included a chart to show you the costs of doing a mailing. Whatever the cost of your mailing, though, your campaign will fail if you ignor the following important factors:

1. A quality mailing package
2. Your mailing list
3. Testing, rolling out and repetition

1. A Quality Mailing Package

One of those factors is how your targeted potential customer will react to your mailing piece. Will your customer send you a check immediately or will he throw your literature in the trash? Our goal is to create a high-quality mailing piece that looks inticing, because the more inticing, the more likely the customer is to open the envelope and read your pitch and send you money.

The testimonial

Potential customers are more likely to believe what one of your previous customers says about your book than what you say about it.

Apart from excerpts from book reviews, the most credible testimonials are in the form of quotes from letters from satisfied customers, followed by their names and addresses. However, to use their names and addresss, you must have their permission, in writing. The FTC requires that you keep the letters on file. A less credible testimonial is the favorable comment followed by the initials of the person who wrote them, and no permission is needed.

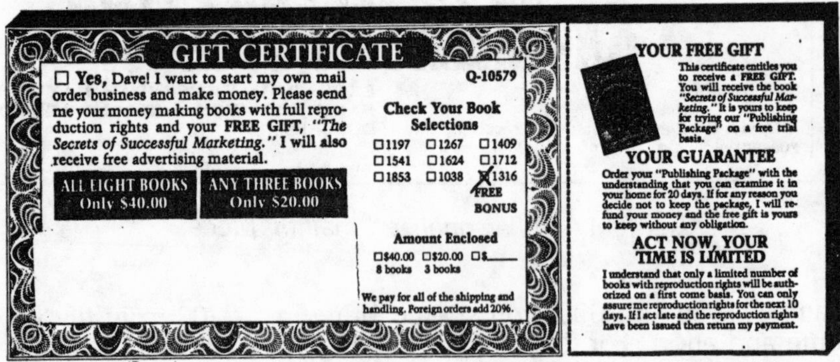

GIFT CERTIFICATE

☐ **Yes,** Dave! I want to start my own mail order business and make money. Please send me your money making books with full reproduction rights and your **FREE GIFT,** *"The Secrets of Successful Marketing."* I will also receive free advertising material.

ALL EIGHT BOOKS Only $40.00

ANY THREE BOOKS Only $20.00

Q-10579

Check Your Book Selections

☐1197 ☐1267 ☐1409
☐1541 ☐1624 ☐1712
☐1853 ☐1038 ☒1316 FREE BONUS

Amount Enclosed

☐$40.00 8 books ☐$20.00 3 books ☐$____

We pay for all of the shipping and handling. Foreign orders add 20%.

YOUR FREE GIFT

This certificate entitles you to receive a FREE GIFT. You will receive the book *"Secrets of Successful Marketing."* It is yours to keep for trying our "Publishing Package" on a free trial basis.

YOUR GUARANTEE

Order your "Publishing Package" with the understanding that you can examine it in your home for 20 days. If for any reason you decide not to keep the package, I will refund your money and the free gift is yours to keep without any obligation.

ACT NOW, YOUR TIME IS LIMITED

I understand that only a limited number of books with reproduction rights will be authorized on a first come basis. You can only assure me reproduction rights for the next 10 days. If I act late and the reproduction rights have been issued then return my payment.

Figure 14.5: Guarantee card

The guarantee card

To be successful, you must gain the potential customer's trust, so you must offer the standard "satisfaction guaranteed" guarantee.

The guarantee can be printed on the flier or the order form, or can be on a separate card with, for example, big headlines and a fancy border. The important things are that your potential customer cannot miss it and that it rams home the idea that there is no risk involved in ordering your book.

The order card

This makes it easy for your customer to order your book and ensures he will not forget to include his name and address. In addition, it is a sales tool and should restate how your book will help your buyer and the terms of the sale. In this card you should summarize the complete sales pitch. Tell the customer what the main benefits will be for him. Some people read only this coupon out of the entire direct mail package, just to find out quickly what the offer is all about.

2. Your Mailing List

The quality of your list is the most important single factor in direct mailing. There are thousands of lists available; for example, the *Direct Mail List and Data Guide* has 25,000 lists available. There are several types of lists and many ways to use them to make money.

The first names and addresses you should enter on your list are those of all your friends, relatives and business acquaintances — anyone who might for any reason buy your book.

The best sources of complete lists are the Yellow Pages, *Direct Marketing* magazine and the Standard Rate and Data Service, which puts out consumer and business lists and the *Direct Mail List Rates and Data* — in effect, about every list available. A listing is free, but subscription to *Direct Mail List Rates and Data* is $80 a year. Your library should have a copy.

Apart from lists, these sources provide names of list brokers, who rent lists to mail order businesses, often for a one-time use. A word of warning: While repetition is a successful tactic, there is a law you should be aware of. If the list you are repeating is your own house list, use it as many times as you like. If the list is a rental, however, you are only allowed to use it once and you cannot copy it — that's the rental agreement and the law.

If one of the names on the list orders from you, you can then add it to your house list. If the list broker catches you using names twice, he will bill you again and may even sue you. There is a good chance he will catch you, too, because list brokers "seed" their lists. Seeding refers to putting dummy names in the list. If your mailer goes to a dummy name twice, the broker knows you used his list twice.

Why go through a list broker if you can get lists directly from the Standard Rate and Data Service? Because a list broker offers you free, expert advice on what lists to use and how to use them. The person who owns the list pays the broker's fee — 15% to 25% of the rental fee; they both want you to succeed because your success means you will be ordering more lists.

The cost of your list is also important. It should be between $25 and $100 per thousand names and addresses; most are between $35 and $45, depending on how hard the list was to compile and how specialized it is.

One company that can help you get the mailing list you need is Hugo Dunhill Mailing Lists Inc., 630M Third Ave, New York, NY 10017. (800) 223-6454 Write or call for a free catalog of the complete selection of lists offered. They will even give you a free guide on making a direct mail piece.

If you would like a list of responsive opportunity-seekers, I can rent my lists to you. If you are interested, write Lion Publishing.

3. Testing, Rolling Out and Repetition

Before committing a large amount of money on a direct mail campaign, you must test your list, unless it is very small or you have no reason to doubt its success.

To test the list, do not rent the entire list. Rather, do the Nth test. This means you rent only every Nth name and address on the list (say, every 10th name) and mail out your package only to those people. This ensures the names you get will not merely be an alphabetical grouping or be of people in one geographical area.

A profitable response to your test will probably be about 2%. A 2% response on a test means that between 1.3% to 2.7% of the entire list will order in response to your full mailing campaign. If you know you can expect a 1.3% to 2.7% response, you can work out if a full-on mailing will make you money.

When you have a successful test, send your mailer to the entire list. This is called "rolling out." If the mailer is not successful, rework your package or pick another list. You will be able to tell the success of your list quickly, because half your response occurs within the first two weeks.

Remember how you code your display and classified ads to measure which are successful? The same applies here — by coding the order form and/or the order envelope, you can tell which mailer and list attracted which responses.

After you've rolled out, consider repetition. If you mail your package to the same list after at least a month, you should get the same response as with the first mailing. The second time round, your potential customers have seen your message twice, and it gets stronger each time. The optimum time period between the first and second mailings is two months.

Your direct mailing piece should arrive on Tuesdays, Wednesdays or Thursdays — these are the days when the least mail arrives and when people spend the most time reading the little that does. In general, December is a bad month for bulk-rate mailing (because of the Christmas rush on the post office); also poor months are March, April, May and June. Good months are January, July, August and September.

Here is a tip: I've found that you can often gauge the quality of a list by the quality of book sold by the person who created the list. If a trashy book was offered, the list usually isn't that good. Personally, I buy the book before I consider buying the list.

Your Own List

You should keep a record of every person who orders from you. These names and addresses mean money to you, whether you rent them to other mail order firms or treat them as potential repeat customers and send them any sales literature you put out in the future.

If possible, store these names on a computer so you can sort and mangage them easily. If you don't have a computer, type them on an Avery Master Sheet, which you can buy at the local office supply store. This sheet has 33 partitions to a page. After you type your labels, have them photocopied on Avery Label Sheets (33 to a page).

When recording your names, always include other information with each label. This information should be kept right above the name. Indicate where the person saw the ad, today's date, the type of book ordered, how much money was sent, and in what form the payment came. Create a code for each of these categories so it is easy for you to place them above each label. Let's go over each one.

"Where the customer saw the ad" tells you where to put your advertising dollars. "Today's date" tells you when your customer's letter arrived.

"How much money sent" has many uses — I use it to tell who has included extra postage for 1st Class mailing and how big a spender the customer is.

"The form of payment" — this is important because you need to know if you can give your customer an instant refund or if you should wait and see if his check clears.

You can invent your own coding system, but here is a typical one:
Money Order = 1, Cash = 2, Check = 3
Use your dept. number for magazine code.
For today's date, use today's date
For payment, use the amount
For type of book, code each book: book1 = 1, book 2 = 2
Sample: 1/MM5/3.25.5/5/3

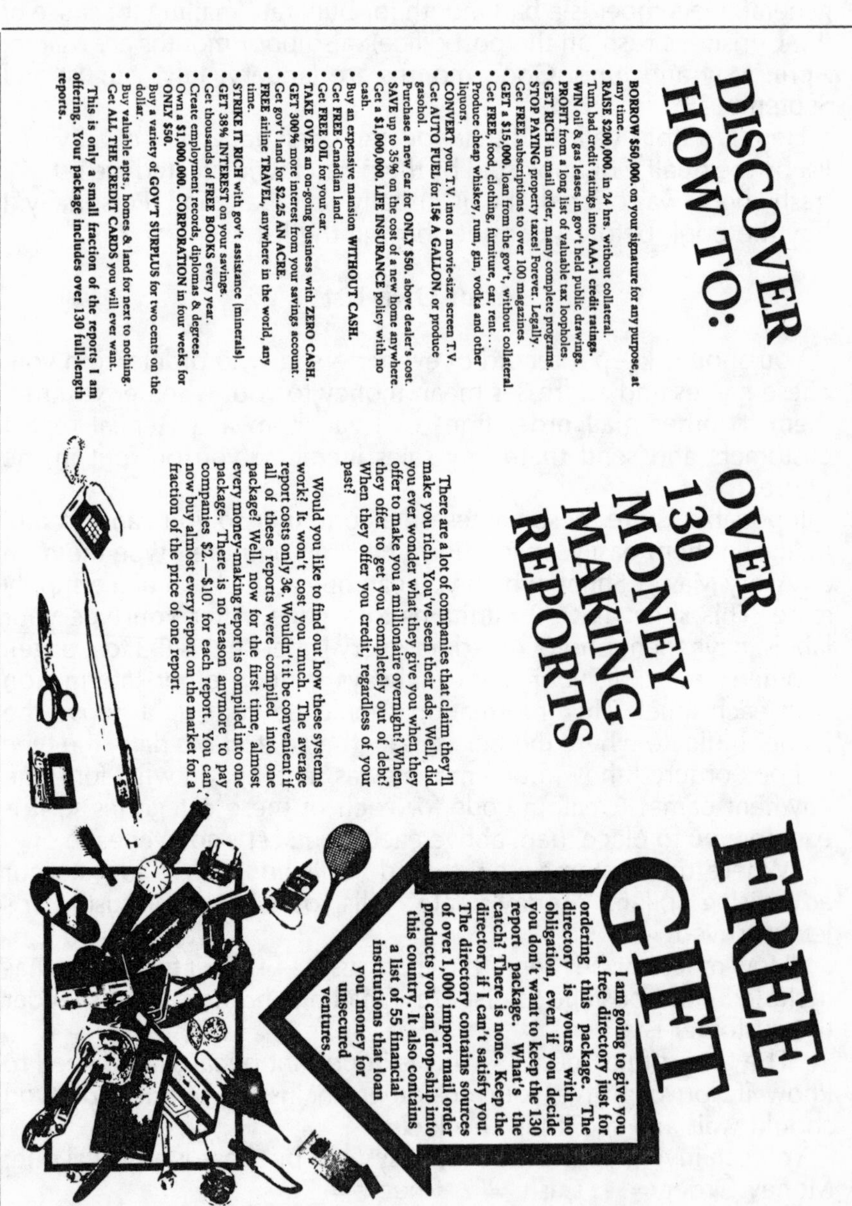

DISCOVER
HOW TO:
• BORROW $50,000. on your signature for any purpose, at any time.
• RAISE $200,000. in 24 hrs. without collateral.
• Turn bad credit ratings into AAA-1 credit ratings.
• WIN oil & gas leases in gov't held public drawings.
• PROFIT from a long list of valuable tax loopholes.
• GET RICH in mail order, many complete programs.
• STOP PAYING property taxes! Forever. Legally.
• Get FREE subscriptions to over 100 magazines.
• GET a $15,000. loan from the gov't, without collateral.
• Get FREE, food, clothing, furniture, car, rent . . .
• Produce cheap whiskey, rum, gin, vodka and other liquors.
• CONVERT your T.V. into a movie-size screen T.V.
• Get AUTO FUEL for 15¢ A GALLON, or produce gasohol.
• Purchase a new car for ONLY $50. above dealer's cost.
• SAVE up to 35% on the cost of a new home anywhere.
• Get a $1,000,000. LIFE INSURANCE policy with no cash.
• Buy an expensive mansion WITHOUT CASH.
• Get FREE Canadian land.
• Get FREE OIL for your car.
• TAKE OVER an on-going business with ZERO CASH.
• GET 300% more interest from your savings account.
• Get gov't land for $2.25 AN ACRE.
• FREE airline TRAVEL, anywhere in the world, any time.
• STRIKE IT RICH with gov't assistance (minerals).
• GET 38% INTEREST on your savings.
• Get thousands of FREE BOOKS every year.
• Create employment records, diplomas & degrees.
• Own a $1,000,000. CORPORATION in four weeks for ONLY $50.
• Buy a variety of GOV'T SURPLUS for two cents on the dollar.
• Buy valuable apts., homes & land for next to nothing.
• Get ALL THE CREDIT CARDS you will ever want.
This is only a small fraction of the reports I am offering. Your package includes over 130 full-length reports.
OVER
130
MONEY
MAKING
REPORTS
There are a lot of companies that claim they'll make you rich. You've seen their ads. Well, did you ever wonder what they give you when they offer to make you a millionaire overnight? When they offer to get you completely out of debt? When they offer you credit, regardless of your past?
Would you like to find out how these systems work? It won't cost you much. The average report costs only 3¢. Wouldn't it be convenient if all of these reports were compiled into one package? Well, now for the first time, almost every money-making report is compiled into one package. There is no reason anymore to pay companies $2.—$10. for each report. You can now buy almost every report on the market for a fraction of the price of one report.
FREE
GIFT
I am going to give you a free directory just for ordering this package. The directory is yours with no obligation, even if you decide you don't want to keep the 130 report package. What's the catch? There is none. Keep the directory if I can't satisfy you. The directory contains sources of over 1,000 import mail order products you can drop-ship into this country. It also contains a list of 55 financial institutions that loan you money for unsecured ventures.

Figure 14.6: Colony Financial Publications insert

Dear Friend,

You've seen those ads in magazines. You know, the companies that claim to make you rich? These companies tell you that they have a system that will make you rich overnight. Don't they all have similar promises? I always ask myself this question, **"If their system is so good, why aren't they using it to make themselves rich?"**

I needed money, and quick. If one of their systems worked, it would be well worth my small investment. You're going to think I'm crazy, but I spent one year buying every report and book that claimed to make me rich. Before I knew it, I had a huge collection of money-making ideas, plans, and systems.

I must have bought hundreds of books and reports on mail order. Many of them were worthless. The good news is that some were good. *I made money with some of these reports.*

With the information in these reports, I got a brand new car (paid with cash), a brand new home, $20,257. in the bank, and I have six credit cards. That is pretty good considering I was about $10,000. in debt just last year.

My friend once asked me how he could raise $50,000. for a store he wanted to open. The banks in town wouldn't give him money. I copied the report I had on getting unsecured loans for ventures, and I gave it to him. He got his loan. Another friend asked me how he could get some credit cards. I made copies of the report on credit cards, and I gave it to him. He got his cards. Before I knew it, people from all over came to me for copies of some of my effective money-making systems.

I once paid $3. for a two-page report on tax loopholes. Could you see yourself paying $1.50 a page? The reports were helpful, but how could companies charge so much for paper? I felt someone had to do something about this situation. My friends convinced me to put together the most valuable reports I had to form a collection of reports. That's exactly what I have done.

I selected 130 of the most valuable reports and put them together in a package for you. Each full-length report was carefully selected to maximize your money-making knowledge. *I have picked out the cream of the crop. Only the reports I felt were of real value are included in the package.* I want to make sure that you are completely satisfied with these reports I have selected for you. **If you don't feel that they are worth at least 100 times what you paid, you will get your money back.**

Not only will you get the reports, but I am going to go one step further. **I am going to give you a free gift just for ordering the reports.** Even if you decide you don't want to keep the reports, the free gift is yours.

The free gift includes a directory of 60 companies that will give you money for unsecured ventures. It also contains a collection of foreign companies that will drop-ship their mail order products into this country for you. Over one thousand import products can be yours for far below wholesale.

You are going to be amazed at the cost of this opportunity. For only $6.00, you will receive over 130 reports, a marketing program, over 100 clip-art pieces, and a free directory.

3¢ each

—ONLY 3¢ FOR EACH REPORT—

Each report is going to cost you about three cents. What can you buy for three cents nowadays?

You're probably asking yourself why the collection of reports is so inexpensive. I had all of the reports typeset into smaller-than-average type. With this professional method, I could save on printing and mailing costs. Why would it matter if they took up fewer pages, as long as they were complete and readable?

Let Me Tell You About My Company

I have served thousands of people in mail order. I've been selling reports for five years now. **Since 1979, I have had over 27,000 satisfied customers.** Pretty good track record, don't you agree?

Now, I only have a limited number of the free directories. You're going to have to order soon. If you order within ten days, I am going to personally guarantee you a directory. Rush your order today.

Sincerely yours,

David Miller

David Miller

(P.S.) I will send you 130 reports, over 100 clip-art pieces, a marketing plan, and a money-back guarantee. The directory is yours to keep, even if you decide not to keep the package. All this for only $6.00! Send for your package today.

Order Today

ORDER FORM

☐ **Yes,** I want to make money with your reports. Send me over 130 full-length informative reports (none less sold) with your free gift directory, reproduction rights, marketing program, over 100 clip-art pieces, and a money back guarantee. Here is my $6.00, send me the whole nine yards.

Name ____________

Address ____________

City/State/Zip ____________

Colony Financial Publications
6065 Mission Gorge Rd., Suite 400
Grantville, CA 92120

Figure 14.7: Reverse of insert

The Self-Mailer and Insert

I must be honest with you. Creating a direct mail package is expensive and beyond the reach of many mail order companies. In many cases it is more cost-effective to create a self-mailer instead of a complete direct mail package.

Say you want your customer to buy $30 worth of books. He doesn't have to spend this amount at once, all on one book. Over time, he may buy several books from you with a total cost of $30. Magazines conduct extensive direct mail campaigns with elaborate packages just to get $10.95 one-year subsciptions. They can afford to do this because they expect renewed subscriptions in the years to come.

There are two types of simple but effective mailing packages: the self-mailer and plain insert. The only difference between the two is that the insert requires an outer envelope; a return envelope is optional. A self-mailer is just a flyer mailed as is — the flyer acts as the envelope. It is a cheaper-looking but cost-effective mailing piece, often used for announcements or to sell low-cost products. Let me tell you more about these mailing packages.

The Colony Financial Publications insert

The insert includes almost everything the complete package contains, but it's all on one brochure. The sales letter, the circular and the order card are all there — be imaginative and see what you can create.

I have an excellent insert created by Colony Financial Publications. Notice how the sales letter is put on one side of the letter, and how the handwriting, done in blue ink, gives it a personal quality. A testimonial is included right in the letter, saying "Since 1979 we have had over 29,000 customers." The order form, found on the bottom right of the letter, summarizes the offer and allows the customer to write his name and address in the blanks.

Turn the page over and you will see the brochure side of this mailer. You can't tell, but all the headlines are in blue. Notice how the biggest benefits are in bold headlines, such as "FREE GIFT" or "OVER 130 MONEY MAKING REPORTS." Right below the headlines, the benefits are elaborated upon. On this side are pictures and lists. Notice the list of subjects of the reports. Believe me, very few people read the complete list. This would make an excellent insert, and inserts tend to get thrown out less often than self-mailers.

15

Free Publicity

The creaters of the pet rock made millions of dollars with their strange toy. Almost every retail outlet carried it. How large do you think the pet rock advertising budget was? Not one cent was spent on advertising. The pet rock was sold exclusively by hundreds of thousands of dollars worth of free publicity. Free publicity is out there, so take advantage of it. Many products become overnight successes because of massive free publicity. Your book can do the same.

Advertising and publicity end with the same result — sales of your book. But there are two major differences: Advertising is expensive, publicity is free; advertising is controlled by you, publicity is controlled by others.

There is one key rule in the self-publishing mail order business: Get as much free publicity as you can.

All publications will accept your publicity package, but only some will use it. Some publications look for unique books, others for those that appeal to a wide audience, and still others for those that cater to the specialized readership that buys their magazine or newspaper.

Types of Free Publicity

There are several kinds of publicity open to you — news releases, feature stories, book reviews, book promotion through magazine articles, and radio and television appearances — and each requires a different approach. I will show you how to deal effectively with each.

News releases

Far more people read news items than read paid ads, and news items lead to publicity and book reviews.

All you have to do is send news releases to all relevant media outlets. Just follow my instructions on how to write a new release — it is easy to do.

Simply type "NEWS RELEASE" and "FOR IMMEDIATE RELEASE" across the top of a piece of your company stationery, then a headline (perhaps the same one you wrote for your display ad, perhaps the title of your book) in capital letters. Double-space on 8½-by-11-inch paper; leave wide margins and try not to exceed one page. Also, you must write in the third person, as if you are a reporter writing about a company. For example, don't write, "We will send you a book." Instead, write, "They will send you a book."

Start with the most important benefit of your book, progressing to the least important (news releases that are not entirely rewritten are often cut off from the bottom to fit available space in the publication).

Explain why the subject of your book is important — is it a resource? Does it deal with a timely or newsworthy topic? Does it contain information everyone must know to survive day to day? Make sure you stress the subject of your book or the issues with which it deals, rather than the book itself — do not make the release seem entirely self-serving or it will end up in the trash. Remember, while the true purpose of your release is to promote your book, it should not appear that way; rather, you should appear to be trying to educate people through a factual, provocative, news-type style.

Include in the release a little background on your book and explain why you are an expert on its subject.

End with the common newspaper cut-off sign, ### or -30-.

Send the release, and, if possible, a black-and-white photograph of the book or one from the book, to appropriate magazines, national and local newspapers, book clubs, wholesalers, libraries, sales

4776 El Cajon Blvd. Suite 204 San Diego, CA 92115

FOR IMMEDIATE RELEASE
Contact: David Bendah
619/265-8777

HOW TO USE YOUR HIDDEN POTENTIAL TO GET RICH

How To Use Your Hidden Potential To Get Rich is a 200-page book that shows people how to use the hidden potential locked in their minds to make a fortune. This book presents a program that clearly maps the route self-made millionaires took to make their fortunes. Any very successful person who has made millions has used the techniques in this book.

Hidden Potential will show any individual, regardless of skill, intellegence and experience, how to use the mind to realize both business and personal dreams.

A complete success program, it is illustrated with charts and diagrams that enable understanding of the mind-transformation process. Included are quizes that monitor the reader's progress to wealth. David Bendah, the author, backs up his points with interesting examples of how ordinary people -- from Milton Hershey to William Colgate -- used the same techniques to make fortunes. Bendah also devotes three chapters to Japanese wealth-building techniques. In short, this volume is designed to expose the reader to every success principle needed to get rich.

Bendah attributes all his success to the principles in his book. Just a few years ago, he was $11,000 in debt and a waiter; now, he has a monthly income of $20,000, rising steadily by 24% a month. He sells 700 copies each month by mail. His book is responsible for creating successful people all over the world.

The 51/2 x 81/2 edition (ISBN-0-933301-00-6) is available from Lion Publishing, 4776 El Cajon Blvd. #204, San Diego, CA 92115, 619/265-8777 for $11.00 (postpaid).

-30-

Photographs of the book and/or author are available on request.

Phone number	Cable address	Telex Address	TWX Address
(619) 265-8777	LION	695 073 Mesa Serv SDG	910 335 1607 Mesa Serv SDG

Figure 15.1: Publicity release

representatives and your alumni, fraternal and professional groups.

In order for the newspaper or magazine to run a picture of your book, you must send a black-and-white glossy photograph of it. If you can, take the picture yourself, with the book standing at an angle just as shown in the example. Make as many copies as you need. Most magazines ask for 8-by-10-inch photos, but send them 4-by-5-inch copies. They can enlarge them if they want to, and you will save on postage and reproduction costs.

For a list of magazines which print publicity releases, check your library or bookstore for *Bacon's Publicity Checker for Consumer Magazines.*

Feature stories

Your local newspaper is constantly on the search for people in your community who have interesting hobbies or jobs, and a published author fits the bill.

Mail your release to the "Features Editor" at the paper; call after a few days to set up an interview.

Not only newspapers will feature you (and your book) in an article — try also your company magazine, national organization publication, college, alumni and fraternal publications and church newsletters. Perhaps there is a special-interest newspaper that reports on the same field as your book. Go for as many as you can — it doesn't hurt to try.

Book reviews

From the author's point of view, there are two phases of the review process, and each is aimed at a different market and demands a different approach.

1. Reviews before publication, aimed at the wholesale market.

Bookstores and libraries must anticipate which books will be in demand before their customers ask for them; to do this, they consult magazines that review books before publication.

Three months before your press run, write a short cover letter addressed to the specific person responsible for book reviews at the relevant publication (current names are listed in *Literary Market Place,* available at the library).

In the cover letter, introduce your book; explain why your book and its subject are relevant to readers; tell the reviewer you hope he enjoys it. With this short letter, send a "galley" of your book (copies of the pasted-up sheets) to the following:

a) Library Journal, Attn: Book Reviews, 205 E. 42nd St., New York, NY 10017.

This highly influential pre-publication review magazine provides excellent exposure, especially for non-fiction works. *Library Journal,* and two of the following publications — *Booklist* and *Choice* — greatly influence which books librarians order.

b) Publishers Weekly, Attn: name of Forecasts editor, Forecasts, 205 E. 42nd St., New York, NY 10017.

Include information on how you plan to distribute and promote your book. This is read by the bookstore industry, and store owners need to know your book will be promoted and draw customers.

c) Booklist, American Library Association, 50 East Huron Street, Chicago, IL 60611.

A sample copy of this review magazine directed at libraries is free on request.

d) Choice, Association of College and Research Libraries, American Library Association, 100 Riverview Center, Middletown, CT 06457.

A sample copy of this magazine, which covers the undergraduate school library market, is free on request.

e) The Washington Post, Book World, 1150 15th Street NW, Washington DC 20071.

f) The New York Times, Daily Book Page, 229 West 43rd Street, New York, NY 10036.

g) CIP Office, Library of Congress, Washington, D.C. 20540.

From the CIP Office, request "Procedures for Securing Preassigned Library of Congress Catalog Card Numbers" and the "Request for Preassignment of LCC Number" application form 607-7. Upon application, you will be given an LC number, which is assigned to your work, as opposed to the ISBN, which is assigned to each edition. You then print that number on the copyright page of your book.

In addition, you should send copies to the major newspapers in your area of the country.

2. Reviews after publication, aimed at the retail and mail order markets.

Once your book is published, you must strive for reviews aimed at the general book-buying public that are published in newspapers and magazines. In addition, you must meet copyright requirements and be listed in as many book lists as possible.

As soon as you have the book in your hands, mail one copy to:

a) Publisher's Weekly, Attn: Weekly Record, 204 E. 42nd St., New York, NY 10017.

b) Library Journal, Attn: Book Reviews, 205 E. 42nd St., New York, NY 10017.

c) Cumulative Book Index, H.W. Wilson Co., 950 University Ave., Bronx, NY 10452.

To get in this important listing, your press run must be at least 500 and your book at least 100 pages long. There is no charge.

d) Register of Copyrights, Library of Congress, Washington, D.C. 20559.

For copyright registration, send two copies plus the fee and application form. I discuss copyright in detail and how you go about getting it in Chapter 4.

e) CIP Office, Library of Congress, Washington D.C. 20559.

f) David Bendah, Lion Publishing, 4776 El Cajon Blvd., Suite 204, San Diego, CA 92115 (And don't forget to autograph it!)

The publications that result in the most sales are, by far, *People, Time, Newsweek, The New York Times Book Review* and the *Wall Street Journal*. But there are many more with book review columns and probably hundreds that may review, or at least mention, your book.

To find these, go to your library and look through the *Standard Periodical Directory,* which lists thousands of magazines, and the *National Trade and Professional Associations Directory* and the *Encyclopedia of Associations,* both of which list professional and trade organizations.

To those with massive circulations or whose interests coincide with the subject of your book, send a copy with the appropriate cover letter and any pre-publication reviews you receive.

To those publications you feel will not readily review your book, send only a "request card" (a card the reviewer fills in and mails to you if he wants a copy of your book).

How to Use Your Hidden Potential to get Rich shows any individual, regardless of skill, intelligence or experience, how to use their mind to realize both business and personal success. It uncovers the route that self-made millionaires took to amass their fortunes. One of the finest books on making money available today. Send $10.00 for a sample copy and dealer details from David Bendah, Lion Publishing, 4776 El Cajon Blvd., Suite 204, San Diego, CA 92115.

Figure 15.2: Book review

Thank any writers who review your book, favorably or not, with a personal letter.

Book promotion through magazine articles

Your book probably contains several chapters and, if it is nonfiction, each chapter probably deals with a different subject, or takes a different slant toward the same subject. Therefore, each chapter, with a little work, can be expanded into a separate piece suitable for magazines.

For example, your book on banking services has chapters on correcting errors on your credit report, establishing credit and various kinds of business loans: each would make a magazine article.

Write to the editors, include a few pages of your book, an outline of the article, and an offer to write the article in the publication's editorial style.

If accepted, you probably won't get paid much, but the exposure will be worth it. Indeed, for some of the smaller magazines, you could offer to write the article for free.

Don't forget to include a blurb at the end of the article stating that you are the author of *Banking* and where it is available.

Radio and television appearances

Nothing will plug your book better than a few minutes on the top television talk shows: *Tonight, Merv Griffin, Phil Donahue, Today, Good Morning America.*

For a list of radio stations that may feature you and your book, look up radio stations with talk shows in *Standard Rate and Data* for broadcast media.

It is easiest to get on small-town radio stations, but you will be featured on the largest stations in the country if you prove to the community affairs producer that your book will benefit his program. Most small cities have at least one local television and radio station that has at least one local talk show.

Write to the community affairs producer; include a press release which finds a local angle to your book, or ties it in with a local, national or international problem affecting the station's viewers or listeners.

When you do get air time, like a good Boy Scout, BE PREPARED. Practice talking about your book beforehand; anticipate likely questions and rehearse their answers. Use words with impact and don't be modest — but don't plug your book at every chance. Address the book's topic, not the book itself.

Good bait to use when writing a letter to the community affairs producer is to ask five questions, to be answered when you get on the air. Get his curiosity going. Tell him you will call him on Tuesday at 9:30 a.m. to set up an appointment. At the designated time, give him a call and persuade him to feature you on his radio show.

Retail Book Sales

The main thrust of this book is mail order book sales. But some authors will want retail book sales as well. To get into bookstores, your book has to be high quality.

If you do decide to sell your book to bookstores, you must do so on a discount schedule and allow for all returns if the bookstore can't move the book. An average wholesale discount to bookstores is 40% to 50%. The bookstores should pay freight costs.

Promoting Your Self-Published Book

The Self-Publishing Manual

Promoting your self-published book is easy if you have a good guide to follow. One of the best books on self-publishing is *The Self-Publishing Manual,* by Dan Poynter. It saved me thousands of dollars when I started publishing books. Informative and complete,

Poynter's 352-page book is a constant reference on the writing, printing, publishing, marketing and distribution of books. If you plan to write and publish soon, you will find this manual invaluable. He covers retail book sales on a larger scale and in more detail than I have. If your local bookstore is out of stock, I will send you a copy within 48 hours for $15 plus $1 to help cover postage and insurance.

16

Good Records, Greater Profits

Bookkeeping

Studies show that as many as 80% of business failures are caused by poor record keeping. Don't make this common error, don't fail when you can succeed — keep records. Simple bookkeeping and record-keeping systems save time and energy and will stop your self-publishing mail order dream from drowning in a bog of paperwork.

You must keep and file records to figure your profits, expenses, taxes and deductions, to control inventory, investigate customer complaints and create mailing lists (which, by the way, can be rented to list brokers, a moneymaker you can tap into that I mentioned in Chapter 14).

Here are some bookkeeping tips:

1. Copy transactions. You should have at least one copy of all transactions, filed either by number, date, customer's last name or by item. I keep a copy of all mailing transactions on a customer label, as I showed you in Chapter 14.

2. Keep calendars. A calendar that shows when goods and supplies have to be ordered and bills paid will help you anticipate and plan for your obligations.

3. File receipts. A good control for listing incoming money is your duplicate bank deposit slip. Include the invoice number and invoice date for each transaction on your deposit slips.

4. Record expenditures. Dating is a good control for money being spent; it allows you to list both your checks and any cash expenditures in chronological order. Pay for as many things as possible by check; if you pay cash, get a receipt.

Customer Records

1. Daily Customer Orders

I am going to show you a simple method of keeping track of all customer orders. You could keep a log for all incoming orders, but that is so time consuming. I fill up to 1,000 orders for books every week. If I didn't have an efficient method, I'd be out of business.

I would like you to review the code I showed you how to create in Chapter 14. It's reprinted here for your convenience:

Money Order = 1, Cash = 2, Check = 3
Use your deptartment number for magazine code.
For today's date, use today's date.
For payment, use the amount.
For type of book, code each book: book 1 = 1, book 2 = 2

Sample: 1/MM5/3.25.5/5/2

The first step is to open the envelope, see what is in it and place the above code on the envelope in red so it is easily seen. Then type the code on a label. Place the code right above that person's name. Then type out 33 labels on an Avery sheet, as explained in Chapter 14. Have it photocopied on label sheets. You then have one master and one sheet of labels. Affix these labels to your mailing envelopes.

By looking at the labels affixed to your envelopes you will know exactly what to send your customer. Fill the envelope and mail it that same day. I do, whether or not the customers' checks clear the bank. Some mail order companies wait up to three weeks for checks to clear. If you are a small company or if the checks are for a large amount, wait until they clear.

As an example, let's use a sample label I've created:

3/MM5/3.25.5/5/2.

For all orders that begin with 1 or 2, send out the books right away because 1 or 2 means cash or money orders were sent. This particular label begins with a "3," which means a check was sent. All you do is add three weeks to all labels that begin with a "3." This particular label gets mailed on 4/14 because the date on it is 3/25.

To calculate how much money you are making and which books are selling, use the master label sheets. Take the data from these sheets and convert it to a revenue ledger. Every single piece of data you need is right on the label. A computer can analyze the code for you.

2. Special Customer System

This system allows you to keep track of your good customers (those who order your books often), and your bad customers (those who send you rubber checks or return your books).

It is important to keep track of your good customers, because repeat business is satisfying and a moneymaker.

Put the names of customers who order from you many times on a preferred label list. Retype their names and addresses as well as their codes on a new label. For example, the label of a prefered customer might be:

3/MM5/3.25.5/25/2.1.

Notice this label indicates the customer bought two books for $25.

Set up cards for each one of your preferred and bad customers. Use a separate card for each buyer. Pick up these cards at your local supply store, or, if you like, reproduce the sample card in this book. On it, have a space for the customer's name and address, the date of first inquiry and the date of first order. As the customer orders more books, log the date, books ordered, prices and total amount of the order, plus any additional information you consider useful. If his check bounces or he returns books continually, note that fact — you'll have to contact him about the bounced check and think twice about filling any more of his orders. More is discussed on what to do about bad checks at the end of Chapter 12.

3. Inventory statement

The inventory status sheet keeps at your finger tips all the information you need about your inventory — how large it is, how much you need and when, from whom you ordered it. You will need this

Figure 16.1

Name ______________________________ Date of order __________

Address ____

City ______________________ State __________ Zip __________

Comments ____

Date	Product Ordered	Price	Total Order

Figure 16.1: Customer cards

only if you have a large inventory.

The more books you sell, the harder it is to fill orders and keep track of inventory. If you find a book isn't selling well, get rid of it. Advertise and keep only the books that make you money. It is better to sell 500 copies of five different books to 500 customers, than to sell five copies of 100 different books to 500 customers. If you get involved in drop-shipping, you will not have to worry about inventories. But if you have a constant inventory, use the sheet I have provided for you.

4. Weekly record of expenses

Use a new sheet for each week, and record all business expenses. Books that include these sheets are available at your local office supply store. At the end of each week, write in the expenses listed on your weekly record of expenses under the proper categories.

The deductible expense categories are, in alphabetical order: Advertising, Bank charges, Car and truck expenses, Commissions, Dues and publications, Insurance, Interest, Inventory, Laundry and

Inventory Statement

Book ______________________________ ISBN# ______________

Edition ______________________ Source ______________________

Size ______________________ Critical reordering# ______________

Replacement time ______________ Cost per book $ ______________

Profit per book $ ______________ Retail price $ ______________

Additional Comments ______________________________________

____

____

Date	Sent out/ordered	# books	Total books	Cost books	Total cost

Figure 16.2: Inventory statement

cleaning, Legal and professional services, Office supplies, Pension and profit-sharing plans, Postage, Rent on business property, Repairs, Shipping, Taxes, Telephone, Travel and entertainment, Utilities, Workers.

For example, the cost of advertising your book in several magazines and newspapers are totaled and put in this column, under Advertising.

Then, go through your weekly record of expenses again and record on this new chart all non-deductible expenses, such as federal income tax and fixed assets.

In the next column, list the total expenses for all the previous weeks of the year (listed on last week's record of expenses). Then add the figure in the "This Week's Total" column to the figure in the previous column — this gives you the "Total to Date." This is the figure you use on your income tax returns.

If you pay for something by cash or credit card, note that here and remember to get a receipt. Tape an envelope to the back of the book and store all cash receipts in it so you don't lose them.

One word of caution if you are deducting car milage — don't forget to write down all your trips. The IRS wants you to write down where you drove and how many miles you traveled. Include a milage diary on your weekly expenses sheet.

Testing Your Ad

Testing the sales-pull of your advertising — whether classified, direct mail or display — is a key to your financial success. Without it, self-publishing and mail order become not a business, but a gamble.

Testing allows you to tell which ads will work before you invest a lot of money in an extensive ad campaign. It also tells you which aspects of your ads are the most effective. For example, does charging $6.50 for your book rather than $10 increase your sales enough to make up the price cut? Does a blue-colored brochure pull better than a red one? These are things you should find out, and on a continuous basis. If you test constantly, keeping track of the pull of every ad you run, you won't waste a penny on advertising.

The type of test you run depends on the type of ads you run. For example, for classified ads, test the wording of your ad and the effectiveness of the magazine you run it in — just code your return address. For display ads, see which size ad and which sales pitch gets the best response — again, merely code your return address. For direct mail, test the effectiveness of one complete mail package against another, or test which parts of a single package are best. Use

Expense Sheet

Week Beginning____________________ Week Ending____________________

Bus. Expenses	Week Total	Total Prior	Total to Date
Advertising			
Bank Charges			
Car Expenses			
Commissions			
Dues & Publications			
Insurance			
Interest			
Inventory			
Laundry & Cleaning			
Legal & Prof. Serv.			
Office Supplies			
Pension & Profit Shar.			
Printing			
Postage			
Rent			
Repairs			
Taxes			
Telephone			
Travel & Ent.			
Utilities			
Wages			

Figure 16.3: Record of Expenses log

the advertising response sheet for your testing.

Advertising response sheet

This record allows you to analyze your ad campaigns and to gauge the success of individual ads. Use the enclosed sheet — you may reproduce it.

What you should test

1. Price

In Chapter 10 on Pricing Your Book, I told you how vital your choice of price is. Although in the standard "price vs. sales" relationship, the number of sales increases as the price lowers, this may not always be the case. For example, lowering your price from $10 to $6.50 can actually reduce your sales because potential customers may think your book is low quality.

To find out the ideal price for your book, you must test. Do this simply by offering different prices in the same ad run in similar magazines. The price that pulls in the most profit, not just the most orders, is the one to stick with.

2. Your list

I discussed in detail in Chapter 14 how to test lists and what response rate you should aim at.

3. One direct mail package against another, varying the components

There are so many components in a direct mail package (sales letter, envelope, brochure, graphics, etc.) that the variety and combination of the elements you can test are endless. I recommend that you test only one element at a time, otherwise the variables are too many and your test becomes meaningless.

Does changing the wording in your sales letter increase sales? Do customers much prefer self-addressed stamped envelopes over just self-addressed envelopes? Does increasing the time limit on a money-refundable offer make a significant difference?

4. The guarantee and terms of payment

Advertising Results

PUBLICATION ____________ ISSUE ____________ ON SALE ____________

KEY ________ SIZE OF ADV. ____________ COST OF ADV. ____________

PRODUCT ADV. ____________ SELLING PRICE ____________ PROFIT ____________

REMARKS ____

PRODUCT SALES					PRODUCT SALES				
No. of Days	Daily No. of Orders	Total No. of Orders	Daily Cash Sales	Total Cash Sales	No. of Days	Daily No. of Orders	Total No. of Orders	Daily Cash Sales	Total Cash Sales
1					33				
2					34				
3					35				
4					36				
5					37				
6					38				
7					39				
8					40				
9					41				
10					42				
11					43				
12					44				
13					45				
14					46				
15					47				
16					48				
17					49				
18					50				
19					51				
20					52				
21					53				
22					54				
23					55				
24					56				
25					57				
26					58				
27					59				
28					60				
29					61				
30					62				
31					63				
32					64				

Figure 16.4: Advertising Results log

The satisfaction-guaranteed, money-back guarantee is a business standard now, and you should stick with it. If you don't offer it, and your competitors do, your potential customers will surely wonder why. However, there are still advantages you can offer your customers, such as not cashing their checks for 30 days so they have a chance to look over your book. This will increase your response, but will also cost you in increased bad checks. Offer the time-delay in one ad and not in another — see if it makes a significant difference to your profits.

You can also offer COD, cash on delivery. This will increase sales, but some customers will inevitably not pay the mail carrier when the book arrives — you lose the postage charge both ways and make no sale. Test to see which offer increases your sales enough to make up for the losses it incurrs. Remember, overall profit is the gauge.

5. Color

Colored brochures always pull better than black-and-white, but does yours bring in enough extra sales to justify the cost? Also, a red-colored brochure may pull better than a green one — the only way you'll find out is to test.

6. Wording of a classified ad

Read Chapter 13 again for a detailed discussion on how to vary and test the wording of your classifieds. Consider running two different ads for the same book in the same magazine to see which ad is best — you can also use this tactic to test small display ads. Because classifieds are the cheapest to buy, they are the cheapest to test.

7. One magazine or newspaper against another

Some magazines are so similar and cater to such similar audiences that ads run in either will be equally effective. But others will vary drastically in their sales pull — just code your address to see which reponses came from which magazine.

Be warned

When testing, you should be aware of these factors.

Make sure your sample mailing is large enough to be representative of the whole population, or at least of the whole specialized audience your book is aimed at.

Also, don't be surprised if identical ads and direct mail packages sent to similar large lists vary slightly in the number of orders they bring in. If you tested again, the difference would probably disappear or favor the other ad.

Testing direct mail packages is expensive, so test only the important aspects. For example, test sales pitch, color and envelope type, but forget envelope and type size.

A Personal Note

I am kept constantly aware of outstanding moneymaking and personal-growth opportunities, and I would be very happy to share my information with you.

If you would like to be kept up to date with the latest opportunities, please send your name and address to me and I'll put you on my personal mailing list.

Good luck!

Appendix

Figure 12.3

Lion Publishing Co.
4776 El Cajon Blvd., Suite 204
San Diego, CA 92115
(619) 265-8777

Order No.

☐ IF CHECKED HERE, THIS IS AN INSERTION ORDER

☐ IF CHECKED HERE, THIS IS A SPACE CONTRACT

DATE

TO PUBLISHER OF

REPRESENTATIVE

PLEASE PUBLISH ADVERTISING OF
FOR

_____ SPACE _____ _____ TIMES _____ __________ DATES OF INSERTION __________

CLOSING:

POSITION				
COPY	CUTS	KEY		
ADDITIONAL INSTRUCTIONS Please do not back up coupon with another coupon			SIZE	
RATE			CIRCULATION	ON SALE
LESS AGENCY COMMISSION ON GROSS	LESS CASH DISCOUNT ON NET		LEFT HAND COUPON	RIGHT HAND COUPON

SPECIAL INSTRUCTIONS:

PLEASE
ACKNOWLEDGE

After publication, please send one complete copy of this issue and two tear sheets of this ad to us.

Order issued by:

Figure 14.1

Your Direct Mail Costs

Use this chart to estimate your direct mail costs.

OPERATION	COST PER 1,000	TOTAL COST
1. Artwork and Creation	________	________
2. Mailing Lists (Rental)	________	________
3. Printing Brochure	________	________
4. Printing Letter	________	________
5. Printing Business Reply Card	________	________
6. Printing Business Reply Envelope	________	________
7. Printing Outer Envelope	________	________
8. Folding Brochure	________	________
9. Folding Letter	________	________
10. Labeling Mailing Piece	________	________
11. Inserting	________	________
12. Tie, Bag, Mail Mailing Pieces	________	________
13. Postage/First/Third Class	________	________
14. Total Cost	$________	$________

	TOTAL COST
15. Cost of Product	________
16. Fulfillment, Shipping, Postage Cost	________

17. Total Fulfillment, Product Cost Per Order—Line 15 Plus Line 16	$________
18. Number of Orders Received	________
19. Total Cost for Orders Received Line 17 Multiply Line 18	________
20. Total Mailing Promotion Costs Line 14	________
21. Overhead—Salaries, Phone, Rent, Etc.	________
22. Total Cost for Refunds	________
23. Total Uncollectables/Selling Price	________
24. Grand Total Mailing Programs Costs Add Lines 19, 20, 21, 22 & 23	________
25. Number of Inquiries	________
26. Per Order of Inquiry Costs Line 24 Divided by Line 18 or 25	$________
27. Cash Received per Order	________
28. Total Cash Received Line 18 Times Line 27	________
29. Total Mailing Program Costs Line 24	________
30. Net Profit for Mailing Program Subtract Line 29 from Line 28	$________

Figure 16.2

Inventory Statement

Book ______________________ ISBN# ______________

Edition ______________ Source ______________

Size ______________ Critical reordering# ______________

Replacement time ______________ Cost per book $ ______________

Profit per book $ ______________ Retail price $ ______________

Additional Comments ______________________

Date	Sent out/ordered	# books	Total books	Cost books	Total cost

Figure 16.3

Expense Sheet

Week Beginning______________ Week Ending______________

Bus. Expenses	Week Total	Total Prior	Total to Date
Advertising			
Bank Charges			
Car Expenses			
Commissions			
Dues & Publications			
Insurance			
Interest			
Inventory			
Laundry & Cleaning			
Legal & Prof. Serv.			
Office Supplies			
Pension & Profit Shar.			
Printing			
Postage			
Rent			
Repairs			
Taxes			
Telephone			
Travel & Ent.			
Utilities			
Wages			

Figure 16.4

Advertising Results

PUBLICATION ______________________ISSUE____________ON SALE__________

KEY__________SIZE OF ADV.__________COST OF ADV. __________________

PRODUCT ADV. ______________SELLING PRICE____________PROFIT__________

REMARKS____

PRODUCT SALES					PRODUCT SALES				
No. of Days	Daily No. of Orders	Total No. of Orders	Daily Cash Sales	Total Cash Sales	No. of Days	Daily No. of Orders	Total No. of Orders	Daily Cash Sales	Total Cash Sales
1					33				
2					34				
3					35				
4					36				
5					37				
6					38				
7					39				
8					40				
9					41				
10					42				
11					43				
12					44				
13					45				
14					46				
15					47				
16					48				
17					49				
18					50				
19					51				
20					52				
21					53				
22					54				
23					55				
24					56				
25					57				
26					58				
27					59				
28					60				
29					61				
30					62				
31					63				
32					64				

Notes

Notes

Notes

Notes

Notes

Notes

Notes

Notes

Lion Best-Sellers

☐	How To Use Your Hidden Potential To Get Rich	David Bendah	$11
☐	Making $500,000 A Year In Mail Order	David Bendah	$12
☐	The Self-Publishing Manual	Dan Poynter	$16
☐	The Complete Guide To Getting Free Grants and Low-Interest Loans	Lloyd Sanders	$6
☐	How To Get Rich In Mail Order	Melvin Powers	$16
☐	Building A Mail Order Business	William Cohen	$21
☐	How To Write A Good Advertisement	Victor Schwab	$15
☐	Logo-Design Service		$15
☐	The Mail Order Clip Art Handbook		$10
☐	How To Start, Expand & Sell A Business	James Comiskey	$16
☐	Reprint rights on eight books		$25

Lion Publishing Company
P.O. Box 151034, San Diego, CA 92115

Please send the above titles. I am enclosing$____________(Postage and handling included; orders shipped out within 48 hrs.) All books come with a full money-back guarantee.

Name ______________________________

Address ______________________________

City/State/Zip ______________________________

The Self-Publisher's Opportunity Kit

The Self-Publisher's Opportunity Kit contains eight interesting books—they've all been tested and are proven sellers. Each book comes with a copyright agreement, which allows you to reprint and sell as many copies as you wish, and complete step-by-step instructions on how to market these books for the greatest profit.

In addition to the eight titles, you get proven-effective classified ads and a sales letter to promote your books.

The eight books are:

1. How To Get Free Grants
2. Importing—Your Key To Success
3. Success On The Job
4. Making A Fortune With Real Estate
5. The Secret Of Raising Money
6. The Millionaire's Secret Of Growing Rich
7. How To Influence People And Win Them Over
8. How To Get $200,000 In Benefits From The U.S. Government

You also receive this guarantee with your *Self-Publisher's Opportunity Kit:* If, for any reason, you are not satisfied with your kit, return it within 30 days for a full, unconditional refund.

Lion Publishing Company
P.O. Box 151034, San Diego, CA 92115

The *Self-Publisher's Opportunity Kit,* with eight books, certificate of reprint rights, step-by-step instructions, sales letter and classified ads, is only $25.
Enclosed is my $25.

Name ______________________________

Address ______________________________

City/State/Zip ______________________________

Use Your Hidden Potential To Get Rich

David Bendah has come out with a book that you will find irresistible. It promises to create wealth and success. He has gone to the extent of mapping out the same route self-made millionaires take to get rich and then illustrates this path in one unique program. His book is so easy to follow—it contains charts, quizes, diagrams and illustrations that make the task of making money simple. He has made a science out of getting rich.

He explains successful techniques with interesting examples of how 37 ordinary people—from Milton Hershey to William Colgate—used them to make fortunes. A unique feature of his book is the rarity of some of his techniques. He boasts of his three chapters devoted to the exclusive wealth-building techniques of the Japanese.

This is what others think of his book:

"Thank you for putting together such a truly excellent book. For the past three months by using your system I made $36,952. That is the best I have done in my life."

—Sam G., Toronto, Canada

"I am making more money than I can ever use. Last month I made $45,287.37—all thanks to the principles in your book. If I can ever help you in any way, please let me know."

—Olajide S., Nigeria

"Your book is one of the best I have seen and studied. But what impressed me most is your sincerity and willingness to help which simply stood out."

—Burt H., Vancouver, Canada

"Thanks a million for the book. I don't like to be without it as I read it and use it often. Here is a check for another book for my wife. Thank you."

—James M., Kalispell, Montana

Lion Publishing Company
P.O. Box 151034, San Diego, CA 92115

If your book can show me how to make big money, $11 is a small price to pay. Send it to me on the condition that I can have my money back at any time.
Enclosed is my $10 + $1 (for postage & handling).

Name ______________________________

Address ______________________________

City/State/Zip ______________________________